HEALING FAMILY PATTERNS

Ancestral Lineage Clearing

for Personal Growth

Ariann Thomas

Ancestral Wisdom Press

www.AncestralLineageClearing.com

Healing Family Patterns
Ancestral Lineage Clearing for Personal Growth

Published by Ancestral Wisdom Press
Ariann Thomas
www.AncestralLineageClearing.com

ISBN: 978-0-615-53894-5

Library of Congress Control Number: 2011916530

Back Photo: Benjemax Studio
Cover Design: Molton Designs, Jennifer Molton

Copies of the book are available through Ancestral Wisdom Press, www.AncestralLineageClearing.com.

Contents

Client Resistance
Ancestor Resistance

PART TWO
The Healing Process

Forward

As a psychotherapist for over 35 years, I have experienced how disruptive family systems can be when transferred from generation to generation due to pivotal choices, trauma and or life- changing decisions. Family systems may have a positive or negative effect for individuals by affecting attitudes, behaviors, parenting, relationships, health and career choices. Fears that are passed on can have a dramatic effect, influencing one's life styles, obstructing belief systems, and strengthening negative parenting styles to maintain dysfunctional systems.

As a psychotherapist, I have worked with students and clients who have demonstrated such behavioral issues. As an adjunct professor I had a student in class who had a family genealogy going back 8 generations to the time the Huguenots came to America. One of his ancestors was a mother who had lost 13 of 14 children en route to America. This trauma resulted in an extremely dysfunctional overprotection pattern. This pattern was transmitted through the family to the student, which then had to be dealt with in the present.

Another client had a relative in an insane asylum during the 17th century, where she was physically and sexually abused. As a survival mechanism, she

tried to become as invisible or as unnoticeable as possible. This client manifested the 'invisibility' qualities in her physical appearance. She was reserved, slim, had forward hunched-shoulders, a flat chest, and a doormat personality. In my practice, we were able through hypnosis to negate the past generational family influence, and she started standing upright with straight shoulders, and became outgoing, assertive and successful.

I also had a client who brought in her pregnant fifteen-year-old daughter. The grandmother, mother, and now the daughter had all become pregnant by fifteen. They were the product of the same oppressive parenting system designed to prevent the teenage daughters from becoming pregnant, thereby creating the very act they feared. I educated the daughter about the oppressive patterns that had invited the behavior resulting in her pregnancy at a young age, and helped changed the parenting behavior of both mother and daughter.

Generational dysfunctional family systems need to be resolved, and, in my experience, there are multiple ways to solve these issues. As a psychotherapist, I have eclectic orientations, techniques, interventions and methods. As a spiritual teacher, I recognize that there are other modalities that can affect individuals and their relationships.

Families create the foundation and building blocks of our character. They are the vehicles, the working ground, for all that we do in life and how we do it. We can be profoundly affected by life-changing decisions made by our ancestors; and, yet, we can do something to change these effects that obstruct and interfere with creating successful relationships. Families are important aspects of our lives and our well-being. Healing family wounds can be beneficial and result in better health and greater happiness. *Healing Family Patterns: Ancestral Lineage Clearing for Personal Growth* offers an alternative method to traditional psychotherapy.

In this book, Ariann Thomas shows us how our ancestors have experienced trauma, adversity and life-changing decisions that may adversely affect us and be or passed down from generation to generation. Ariann weaves in her own life stories as well as those she guided through the Ancestral Lineage Clearing process with their experiences. She illustrates how aspects of the self—mental, emotional, physical and spiritual—all interact to create who we are. The case histories are intriguing and demonstrate the effectiveness of the method.

The book goes through the theory and application of healing family patterns clearly and interestingly to keep the reader's attention. The book lays out a program of clearing negative patterns in an insightful and straightforward manner. I recommend it to those readers interested in reviewing and healing their personal family histories and patterns.

Rob (Ralph) Robinson
MA Psychology, Licensed Psychotherapist (Retired)

DD (Doctor of Divinity)
2011 at Sedona, AZ

Rob Robinson has been a psychotherapist with a holistic/transpersonal approach for over 35 years with a private practice and experience as a clinical director for 17 years in a popular counseling and training agency for interns in California. The State of California certified Rob for conducting seminars, presentations and workshops for Continuing Education Credits for professionals. Rob was also an Adjunct Professor at Santa Clara University, CA.

Introduction

Welcome to *Healing Family Patterns: Ancestral Lineage Clearing for Personal Growth*. This book is the outgrowth of the continuing search for healing and personal growth in my own life. I came from a typical Midwestern American family with its unique idiosyncrasies. My parents did the best they could to raise eight children (one boy and seven girls) within a nuclear family after World War II. Much of my story is told throughout the book.

After I grew up and left the family, I journeyed to many parts of the country for school and work. I learned many facts, and had my share of success and pain. The knowledge I gained in school and at work helped me manage my way in the material world of business, as well as managing my finances and running a house. Emotionally I was a mess. I adopted many of my family's coping mechanisms of co-dependency, addiction, martyrdom, lack of self-esteem, poverty-consciousness and other patterns that crippled me in seeking personal happiness.

About twenty years ago, a history of generational sexual abuse came out in my family. Because of my background and training as an attorney I recognized the symptoms of sexual abuse, so I was not totally surprised. This revelation created an upheaval and split in the family that was unresolved even years later at the time of my parents' death. Although I was not directly involved, I was certainly affected by the atmosphere of shame, secrecy, abuse and trauma.

As a result of this family pattern I held an unconscious belief that nothing would go right for long, and that something disastrous would always lie ahead to take away my happiness, success and achievement. This was a major stumbling block in my life. After much soul searching, I cried out during a meditation for Spirit to help me.

Spirit honored me with the gift of a meditation that later became this process of Healing Family Patterns, which I call Ancestral Lineage Clearing. It helped me understand the sexual abuse history in my family and, more importantly, to release the energy from my body and other energy systems so I could be free of the trauma. I could then forgive my parents, grandparents and the other relatives involved. I came to value my family and the ties to my past. I saw how my past had shaped my life, my views, my choices and my present happiness.

Healing Family Patterns is a natural outgrowth of my journey of learning, exploration and deep spiritual healing. I have healed my body, mind and spirit, using Western medicine, chiropractic, alternative medicine, psychology, sound medicine, crystal healing, soul retrieval, symbols, energy work, Reiki, massage, Rolfing, Healing Touch, and a variety of other techniques and modalities. All of these have been useful and effective in their time and place.

What I have learned from my own healing is that all healing comes from within. When we heal our hearts, we heal our bodies. So, how do we do this? One of the first places to start is with the family. The family is the model of our inner self. It is the representation of our Sacred Feminine (the mother) and Divine Masculine (the father) energies as represented by our parents.

The Sacred Feminine is the Mother principle of nurturing, caring, healing, holding space for growth and all possibilities, holding safety and security, the warmth of home and hearth—the holder of unconditional love. The Mother Love principle gives us the place to learn and grow at our own pace, in a holistic way, seeing, hearing, tasting, touching and feeling. It is sensuous, in the "now," verbal, right-brain, creative and expansive.

The Divine Masculine is the Father principle of action, creation, motivation, stimulation, focus, encouragement, aggression, thinking, engineering, linear thinking and action, development, left-brain, accomplishment and achievement.

When we are children, mothers try to keep us from climbing the tree lest we get hurt; fathers encourage us to climb higher to test our skills and courage. We need both reasonable limits and enthusiastic encouragement.

When the family is balanced and harmonious, their creation—the children—are happy, productive and creative. When the Sacred Feminine and Divine Masculine are unbalanced and are not in harmony, then strife, unhappiness and unhealthiness result.

Since our Western culture has not recognized or valued the Sacred Feminine for many generations, most of us have come from homes that have experienced this imbalance. Once we heal our family history at its core we are open to experience the happiness and joy that comes from the balance between the Sacred Feminine and the Divine Masculine.

We need to find both aspects within ourselves before we can build a strong family with happy and creative children. By healing our family patterns we begin to create this inner balance and pass it along to our children, grandchildren, and those generations who follow after us.

My purpose in writing this book is to help you, the reader, heal those family patterns that are interfering in your present life, so that you can reach greater joy, health, prosperity and love in your life. My other purpose is to heal the rift within each of us between the Sacred Feminine and Divine Masculine that creates such negative family patterns. When we heal individually, our families also heal.

Great Spirit, God, Creator, the Universe, All That Is or whatever name you give to the Almighty wants us to live our lives to the fullest. Spirit has given me this gift and I pass it on to you in love and gratitude.

To your healing, happiness and joy,
Ariann Thomas
Cottonwood/Sedona, AZ

October 1, 2011

Disclaimer

I want to clearly state at the outset that the opinions, methods and techniques in this book are all mine. They are my OPINIONS. *Healing Family Pattern: Ancestral Lineage Clearing for Personal Growth* is about an energetic healing system and is not intended to treat present physical, mental or emotional illness or dis-eases. It is based upon my own personal experience and the experiences of my family, friends and clients over the years.

I am saddened that in our culture that the government must intrude into the healing relationship between healer and client. I believe we are coming into the time when many of us are taking personal responsibility for our lives and our healing. However, having said that, I still want to ensure that I undertake my responsibility to meet the requirement of the law for whenever the term *healing* appears.

That said, *Ancestral Lineage Clearing has not been evaluated by the FDA and is not intended to diagnose, treat, cure or prevent any disease. Continue seeing all medical and mental health care practitioners and taking prescribed medications while reading this book, having sessions or practicing the techniques described in this book.*

Acknowledgements

I am sure all new authors struggle through their first book, in an attempt to put the ideas in our heads into words on the page that accurately convey the meaning and feeling of what we want to share with the reader. Friends, family and professionals are absolutely indispensable to this process. Without the following people to listen, comment, keep me on track, encourage, support and love me, this book would not have been completed.

I first want to thank my dear friend, heart-sister, mentor, business partner and co-founder of the New Dream Foundation, Misa Hopkins, for all of her wonderful support throughout the years as she listened to my dreams, meditations, and to stories of my ancestors, word struggles, health issues and life processes. She is the ideal friend.

I would like to thank my family members who have so graciously allowed me to use their personal stories in this book: my sister, Julie, and my brother, Gordon, as well as the rest of my sisters who are not mentioned by name.

In addition, there are those steadfast friends who patiently listened to me, who were my guinea pigs in the beginning, or who reviewed those really rough drafts and gave me great feedback: Mira Steinbrecher, Barbara Fasanella, Krystalya Marie, Cindy Mills, Kim Wright, Kelly Cole, Judy Cole,

Davina Snowden, Elizabeth Page, Karen Howell, Finbarr Ross, Silas Robinson, Jeffrey Burger, John Brown, Sandi Weber, Richard Mack, Susan Amari Gold, Suzanne McQueen, &Valerie Olmstead, NMD.

I owe a great debt to my students who helped me find the *holes* in the first draft, and who definitely pushed me to discover better explanations and discussions to clarify certain concepts.

To my clients, I want to express my heartfelt appreciation for the courage it took to look for your ancestors and heal the family patterns that were present for generations. You are the ones who are healing the planet. I honor you with this book.

I also gratefully acknowledge the wonderful professionals who offered their expertise to make this a quality product:

Rob (Ralph) Robinson, M.A., D. D. (Divinity), psychologist and psychotherapist, spiritual teacher, and good buddy, who reviewed the manuscript and wrote the Forward;
Sharon Hooper, my dear friend and outstanding editor;
Barbara Dulmage, Ph.D., editor extraordinaire;
Benjamax Studio and Terri, for the lovely portrait photograph
Jennifer R. Molton, Molton Designs, my patient pal and graphic designer; and
Ixchel Tucker, my long-time spirit-sister and web designer.

PART I
Healing Family Patterns Through Ancestral Lineage Clearing

Chapter I
Healing Family Patterns: Using Ancestral Lineage Clearing to bring Greater Health, Wealth and Love into your Life

Present World Transition and Personal Crises

At this time in our history momentous events are occurring. There are natural disasters of unusual power, frequency and strength, as well as global warming and weather changes, world-wide financial crises, political upheavals and personal re-evaluations. I have found that when the world seems to be more chaotic than usual, we all tend to look inward for healing our personal lives since the world seems out of control.

As the world transformation approaches and continues in this challenging time, I believe humanity is feeling an intuitive need to clear out stale, negative and unhealthy energy, and seeks a new way of living in love and harmony. Innumerable healing books, techniques, modalities and theories bound today, because we are searching for ways to heal our bodies and our spirits.

Many healing modalities such as herbal remedies and meditation available today have been around for thousands of years, while it seems others are discovered daily. The medical community appears to discover new *dis-eases* all the time—or, perhaps just continues to improve in diagnosing the body's discomforts.

Often when life seems overwhelming, illness, financial problems and relationship malfunctions become more obvious. Healing our lives tends to become a priority.

By healing our own lives we become the very solution to the world's problems. As we heal ourselves, we heal those around us, thereby healing the cause of conflict and distress within the Earth and in others. The more peaceful and joyous our lives become, the more we spread peace and harmony throughout the world. The great philosophers and masters of the world have been teaching this concept for centuries.

The technique of Healing Family Patterns (also called 'Ancestral Lineage Clearing') as explained and set out here is one of a number of healing modalities for your own personal growth. However, the stories from the sessions with my clients are the most valuable part of this book. Actual accounts of clients' journeys into their ancestors' past and how their family patterns were changed as a result of this healing method will show how this healing method truly works, though the clients' names and all identifying information have been changed to protect their privacy.

I hope you will find this process beneficial for your life, too.

Family Patterns—Choosing Your Original Family
We all choose our families before we incarnate on earth. Family is both the most important gift and the greatest obstacle in our lives. The most important and deepest healing takes place around issues concerning families.

Despite all its challenges, the family of your childhood is always your greatest gift. You are who you are today because of this family.

The one commonality everyone in this world shares is family. Most of us know our biological family and grew up with them. Some did not. We all have a family of some type, even though we may be separated, estranged or removed from the family into which we were born or with whom we grew up. Even if we do not know our biological family, we were probably raised with another family, whether an adoptive family or a foster family.

There are many different kinds of families, from small nuclear families of one parent and one child, to huge extended families of numerous relatives, including grandmothers and grandfathers, aunts and uncles, brothers and sisters, cousins, nieces and nephews, all living and growing up communally.

Some grew up rich or poor, loved or abandoned, in a home or on a street, well fed or half-starved, educated or ignorant, hard-working or lazy, healthy or ill, somewhere on this earth.

No matter how, where or when we grew up, our family of origin and the primary family that raised us had a tremendous impact on who we are now, what we believe, our present values, our health, our attitudes toward work, marriage, children, relationships, religions, and a myriad of other things great and small in our lives.

To a large degree our attitudes about satisfaction with life, happiness with family, loving relationships and self-image, come from our early training and the messages we received from our parents. If we received validation and love in our early years, then the world is a wonderful place waiting for us to make our mark. If we were abused, neglected, dismissed, ignored or put down, then our self-image and our view of the world are distorted.

Healing family patterns around issues and challenges that are common to family members frees a tremendous amount of energy for all family members and allows multiple people to heal at one time.

Healing Family Patterns through Ancestral Lineage Clearing to Improve Our Lives

Healing Family Patterns by requesting help from your ancestors is not a new technique. It has been practiced for hundreds, if not thousands, of years in other cultures under different names. Buddhists have a specific ritual to remove the negative influence from ancestors. A ritual called Shadow Removal has been practiced for hundreds of years in rural areas of Latin and Caribbean countries. And, a variety of Shamanic practices are done under an assortment of names.

Many psychologists use a similar technique in dealing with family pattern emotional issues. Although not similar in process, it is comparable to Hellinger Family Constellation Dynamics. I have recently learned of a similar process called Resetting Family Patterns. This tells me that others have also recognized the value of getting in touch with old family issues to heal present ills.

`The process I have developed along with other similar practices is called Ancestral Lineage Clearing.

How Healing Family Patterns and Ancestral Lineage Clearing Started

So, how did I learn to heal my family patterns by the process I now term 'Ancestral Lineage Clearing'? I discovered this healing method when I asked for help from Spirit during a meditation.

I began my healing journey in my late 20s and early 30s after completing undergraduate and law school and getting my first job. I suffered from migraine headaches in law school from stress, overwork and probably reading too much. I was getting two to three migraines a week with visual and auditory distortions. I lost 25 pounds in 3 months as a result of the nausea and lack of appetite.

While in school I went to the medical teaching hospital for the headaches. After running numerous diagnostic tests, the doctors gave me daily medication for classical migraines and sent me on my way. I decided I was not going to live my life dependent upon medication, so when I started working I found a M.D. who taught me bio-feedback and auto hypnosis, which later morphed into a daily meditation practice.

Throughout the following decades, I continued to study other alternative healing methods such as Healing Touch, Reiki and various forms of energy. After a health crisis in my 40s left me disabled with joint problems, chronic pain and depression, I continued to investigate alternative healing techniques. Without a daily practice of meditation, exercise, supplements, medication and various alternative healers, I would still be non-functional and housebound today.

One of the most profound insights I discovered on my healing journey was that I must take responsibility for my own healing. No one can heal me. I can only heal myself.

True healers from every culture absolutely believe this and empower their patients with this belief. Not all health providers necessarily support this belief.

After years of exploring various physical, mental and emotional healing modalities, I felt there was still something missing. I had some deep emotional issues that were preventing my complete physical healing. I had used psychological and spiritual therapy, soul retrieval, past life regression, sound medicine, life readings, astrology, massage, cranial-sacral work and other forms of therapy; however, these healing methods could not seem to reach some core issues.

During these years I found a deep spiritual connection with the Native American traditions. As I am part Cherokee, the Native Way appealed to me. So, in I cried out for help and guidance from Great Spirit, the Divine, Creator one of my meditations, God, or whatever you may choose to name the Source.

I understood at the time that some issues were deeply rooted in our family history. These matters became entrenched until they were established family patterns. We often fail to recognize these family patterns because everyone around us lives their lives within that pattern. For example, if everyone in your family eats dog food, you think it is normal to eat dog food until someone shows you differently.

For several months I had been feeling restless and anxious. I knew from past experience that this was a precursor to a healing breakthrough of some type. I also felt that the next healing step had something to do with my family.

About twenty years prior I learned about the generational sexual abuse prevalent in my family. My maternal grandfather had abused my mother, and my maternal grandfather, uncle and my father had then abused several of my sisters. I also suspected involvement of other family members that had not been confirmed. During this same period, I was having a number of dreams about my deceased parents and other family members.

The disclosure of sexual abuse had devastated our family and torn it apart. At the time of my father's death, out of eight children, only one sister and I had been in communication with our parents. And, at the time of my mother's death, I was the only child who was speaking to her.

Although I had not been part of the sexual abuse pattern, I had recently uncovered memories of early pre-verbal physical abuse. I had of course also been affected by the sexual abuse of others in the family; and, even though I did not believe that for years, I learned otherwise.

I had been meditating regularly for 25 years, initially to reduce pain from migraines. One day while meditating, I asked Spirit to show me what I needed to learn. I went into a deep, deep meditation, and journeyed into the past.

(For years I had understood and believed that time was not linear and I studied quantum mechanics theory as a layperson. However, I confess that the mathematics of quantum mechanics is way beyond my comprehension.)

I instinctively sought the person with whom, or where, the sexual abuse and domination had originated in the family. In my meditation, I saw a gathering of women in a forest. They were dressed in long dresses or skirts of a very long time ago. I knew intuitively that it was in Europe, about 450 years ago.

The Women's Curse

The women came individually into the clearing, secretly, silently, in the shadow of the full moon. The group had done this before many times and they knew each other well.

An elder spoke:

"She is dead. They hanged her today."

Several women burst into tears; there were gasps of outrage from others, and still others moaned in despair. Someone (me?) stepped forward and said,

"Alright, now is the time for us to decide what to do. Killing Alea is just the beginning. If the men feel we are a threat to their power to such an extent that their only recourse is to lock us up or take our lives, we must protect ourselves and our daughters."

There was much discussion and arguing about whether it was only Alea's vicious husband behind the hanging, or whether the men of the town had supported him in having her declared a witch so he could get his hands on her property, which she controlled with an iron fist.

Her husband had always felt useless because of her money, so he had beaten her. Since she had been born into a wealthy family and looked down on others, she was considered arrogant. The men generally sided with her husband, so when he accused her of witchcraft, others took up the cry and no man would defend her. The Sheriff used this as an excuse to condemn her to death and to teach the women a lesson to stay in their rightful place.

The mood of the world was shifting against women healers, holy women and property owners. The church, the judicial system and the king seemed to be slowly altering the laws and the political system to strip whatever independence women had. Even widows could no longer reside in their husbands' homes without the consent of their sons.

Rumors came from far away that women were burned as witches for healing with herbs and potions. If this were so, many in their gathering who kept the rites of the Ancient Goddess of the Moon, though Christian too, were likely candidates for burning or hanging.

I knew my husband loved me, but he greatly preferred our sons over our daughters. He would gladly leave all the property to them if he could, leaving our daughters to the mercy of whatever their husbands would do, good or bad.

The welfare of women was not considered by the men in their creation of laws and by the churches' edits. They cannot protect other women from the injustices of weak men who beat or bully their wives and children, or leave them to starve. If the good men cannot protect women, then we must protect ourselves.

After what seemed hours of discussion, we decided it was time to call upon the Goddess to protect us and our daughters.

We pooled our energy and called upon the Goddess that night. We demanded that women be able to influence men to care for and protect us and our daughters.

11

We pleaded for the power of our most potent weapons: our bodies. Through sex and sexuality we wanted to control and convince men to do what is right, fair and just and to help us care for others who could not care for themselves. We asked that this power be transferred from us to our daughters, and to our daughters' daughters, and on down to the women of generations to come.

The women basically asked for the power to manipulate men out of their own fears of death, destruction, poverty and helplessness.

Then I saw the situation backfire. In future generations some women only had sons, so the *curse*, power or influence passed on to the men. The men obtained the power to manipulate without the consciousness of the powerlessness of women behind it. These men, too, feared death, destruction, poverty and helplessness. Again, they took their fears out on women. They used the sexual power of manipulation to control and subjugate women even more so. **But** the situation **originated with us,** the women in the circle.

The irony was that the cure of sexual manipulation began in an attempt to protect women, and turned into another form of abuse. I knew as well that manipulation of anyone for another's purpose, no matter what the intent, interferes with the other's free will and is wrong.

As I came out of the meditation, I prayed to the Goddess to lift the *curse, protection prayer* or whatever it was called, and to restore balance between men and women in my family. I clearly heard the Goddess say *yes* with a smile in her voice.

After this meditation and the clearing of my energy, I felt so much better. A great weight was lifted from me. The restless and anxiety was gone. My fatigue was better and I had much more energy.

I asked myself: was this real? Was this a dream or wishful thinking? Or, was this just Spirit's way of showing me a vision of how it *might* have happened, and then a way for me to clear it energetically from my field? I didn't know what to think.

About three days later, one of my younger sisters, Julie, called me. A powerful healer in her own right, she asked me, "What have you been doing? Have you been doing some healing work lately?" She didn't know that I had done this ancestor clearing. She went on to tell me that she had felt 'something' shift about three days earlier. She didn't know what had happened, but she was feeling better, lighter and clearer. Julie lives about 1500 miles away from me.

Julie was also working with a healing therapist at the time, dealing with issues arising from the family sexual abuse issue. When she had her next session during which the issue arose, the therapist began following the energy they had been working on and told her, "Oh, that's been cleared up. We don't have anything else to do there. Yes, it looks like it was about 400 years ago. It's done. We can move on . . ." So, even her therapist verified that the energy had been cleared.

This confirmed to me that Ancestral Lineage Clearing worked, and that others could feel the results when the energy was cleared from the person's energetic field and their body. I was very excited as I continued to practice returning to my ancestors to clear out family issues that were affecting me as well as other family members.

I had been working with crystals for almost 20 years and began using crystals to hold and maintain the new energy as I cleared out the old energy patterns. My lineage clearing system was quickly developing. I began to 'practice' on friends, doing lineage clearing on their issues. It was fascinating to see how quickly and efficiently the process removed stuck patterns.

About two months after the initial clearing, I got a call from a friend who referred her friend, Kathleen Casey, to me. Kathleen was coming to Sedona to do a workshop on Ancestral Lineage Clearing. She needed a local reference and contact, and would I mind if she gave Kathleen my number? What synchronicity! Well, there are no coincidences, so I quickly assured her that I would be happy to help Kathleen set up a workshop in the Sedona area.

I knew immediately that Kathleen and I would be friends after our first contact by phone. She was such a delightful person, and we promptly began exchanging information about how we did our lineage clearing. She had been doing clearings for ten years. I had just started!

Kathleen is a marvel. She generally works with groups, using a very intuitive and co-creative process, although she does individual sessions too. We use the same basic format of meditation and journeys to contact the ancestors. In addition to her voice, she uses a remarkable gong and multiple musical instruments to break the old energy patterns and to establish the new energy in the energy fields of her clients after the old patterns have been broken. She is incredibly talented in assisting people through their issues, particularly in group settings.

Working with her was a pleasure and we traded histories of our experiences, though our methods were basically pretty similar. As a result of our exchange and the co-facilitating, she decided to incorporate crystals into her program and I decided to use more sound in my clearings. I continued to explore how to release the old ancestral energy from my energy field and discovered sound to be most effective. Now I use toning and sound to clear old energy.

Conclusion

Now is the time for joy and happiness to return to the planet. New or forgotten methods of Healing Family Patterns, such as Ancestral Lineage Clearing, are being rediscovered and brought forward for our use in this time period.

We are all created with the ability to heal. Healing negative family patterns frees energy that has been trapped in our bodies and spirits since childhood, and bound in families for generations. Once released, we are able to create life anew and fill

15

it with happiness. Sometimes all we need is a little assistance and direction.

Chapter II
Evolving the Ancestral Lineage Clearing Method

After doing Ancestral Lineage Clearing for about six months I found the energy clearing method evolving and changing. After working with this vision for several months I discovered the next step, which was to **shift the energy in the past**. It was an amazing revelation.

The Next Step in the Clearing Process

One day a client, Angela, came to me for a session concerning her relationships with men. All of the women in her family had had men who left in one way or another: they died of illness or disease; they were sailors who were frequently absent; some had abandoned their families; others had died in wars or departed in some other way. She knew of no family in her lineage in which a father had been present in the lives of his children as they grew up.

We began the session by searching for the ancestor who began the pattern.

Absent Husbands

Angela stepped out of the time stream into a bright, warm, sunny afternoon in a city several centuries ago. She saw a woman in the courtyard of a small two-story Italian stucco home. The courtyard bordered on the river where there was a landing dock. Two small children played around her as she hung the laundry. She sang a happy tune while she worked. This was clearly her ancestor.

A boat pulled up at the landing dock and a young man dashed up the steps, grabbed her hands and said, "Maria, your husband is dead. As we were loading the boat the wood slipped, and he tried to save the other men and the boat. He was hit on the head. When we pulled him from the water he was dead."

Maria dropped to her knees and began to keen. This frightened the children, who ran to her, and they began crying, too. The young man was their uncle, Maria's brother-in-law. He tried to comfort them. He knew Maria had loved his brother very much, and there was no comfort for her at this time.

After her husband's death Maria was forced to marry this 18-year-old brother-in-law. Neither particularly wanted the marriage, but this was the custom and an unwritten law.

In order to keep the business in the family and protect the widow and her children, the closest single, male relative married her. The assets were then transferred to the man since a woman could not own property.

Maria resented her brother-in-law, now her husband. She became a shrew, constantly nagging him and comparing him to his older brother, in business, as a father, and as a husband and lover. He felt incompetent, unloved and emasculated. She even turned the children against him, so they, too, mocked him at every turn. After about ten years he fled, abandoning them for a new life elsewhere. Maria never heard from him again.

After they grew up her children left her, too. Her son moved away and her daughter married and rarely visited. She died a lonely and embittered old woman.

As the clearing progressed and while we were still in the past with her ancestor, I realized the **energy from the past needed to be shifted.** Even if we cleared the energy in the present, Maria was still living with the consequences of the choices she had made in that life.

I requested that Angela ask her ancestor if she was willing to change her life and alter her choice.

The ancestor said yes. I then requested that Maria go to the point in her life when she might have made a different choice that would have altered the outcome of her life. I later defined this as *the **Choice Point***.

Maria immediately went back to the time of the marriage to her brother-in-law. She knew he was young and hoped to make a better marriage, but he chose to do his duty toward her. She could not yet love him, for she still loved her deceased husband. She decided to accept the situation for the sake of the family. She began by treating him with kindness. In return, he was good to the children and to her.

He took over the business, and, with her help, it was put it back in order within a mere matter of months. In a few years they grew to love and understand each other. It was not the grand passion of her first marriage, but the gentle and warm love of a mature and fulfilled woman.

Her husband appreciated the richness and support he had found in a good woman, and a warm and loving home. The children accepted their new father and loved him totally. He grew into maturity and became a respected member of the community.

Maria died happy, surrounded by her husband, her children and her grandchildren. Her life had been filled with love, fulfillment and joy.

We brought this energy forward into Angela's present lifetime.

We asked the ancestor from that past lifetime to choose a different *probability stream* from the actual one she had chosen in her lifetime. Then we carried the energy of the **new probability stream forward into this lifetime.** This new energy was perfect for Angela to break her family pattern. She could now look forward to establishing a long-lasting relationship with a partner who would choose to stay with her.

After this session I used this technique on my own next lineage clearing. It was absolutely clear to me that I had found a **key to altering the energy in a substantive way.**

When the energy was changed in the past with the original ancestor, the alterations went directly to the heart of the issue. I could bring the **new energy from the second lifetime of the ancestor directly into the present.**

When we came back from the journey, it was a simple matter to release the old negative energy from the first lifetime, and incorporate the new

21

energy the ancestor had already chosen, knowing the outcome was positive and the negativity cleared.

Now when I take a client into the past, I ask the client to go to the ancestor who carries the energy of the issue affecting the client's life. After this ancestor identifies the circumstances that "created" the challenge, the ancestor makes a different choice in his or her life that results in happiness. The client's life is now free to receive the new positive energy. **I have never had an ancestor refuse to** make **a different choice.**

Using this Gift for Others

As I continued to explore the breadth and depth of this healing method, I was constantly surprised by the usefulness and ease with which Ancestral Lineage Clearing can handle any type of issue. I realized this was a gift I could share with others.

Take a moment to consider: if you have a brother or sister who asked you for advice about their first date, wouldn't you try to make it easier for them? If you had/have a child, don't you want them to be happy? Wouldn't it be great if they were popular and got good grades?

Why should we consult our family ancestors? Because our families, parents, grandparents, siblings, cousins and other relatives **love us and wish us well**. Every generation wants subsequent generations to be happy and successful.

Family Obstacles

In addition to the wonderful gifts we received from growing up in whatever family we had as a child, we all realize by adulthood that we may have received some not-so-wonderful gifts (at least in our eyes). I always wanted to be an only child rather than of one of eight. When my only-child friends hear of my multiple siblings, they breathe, "Oh, it must be wonderful to have brothers and sisters." It is all about one's personal perspective.

However, there are some definite physical, mental, emotional or spiritual attitudes, values, beliefs or leanings that we discover later in life, which may result in undesirable traits in our present life. Alcoholism, poverty consciousness, abuse, anger management, fear, religious intolerance, racism, self-destructive tendencies, negative self-images, work-related issues, responsibility issues, destructive attitudes, and negative world views, are just a few of the many issues that can arise from early upbringing and family traits.

Sometimes we attempt to break away in our teens and twenties only to fall back into the family trap of guilt, shame and abuse. Many times these tendencies are unconscious, so we are not aware of them unless we continue to repeat them until the pain becomes intolerable and we can no longer refuse to face them. Then we recognize the pattern and realize, "Hey, I'm doing the same thing Mom always did to Dad." Or, "That's why Dad always worked late: so he didn't have to face decisions about the finances at home." Recognition that our patterns relate to family issues is the first step in healing dysfunctional behaviors in our own lives.

Family Gifts

Once we uncover the family patterns that negatively impacted our lives and altered them, we often begin to recognize the family gifts that have freed us from some of the issues besetting others. Are you successful at work? Your success may rest on family foundations of good work ethics and values. Is your body strong and healthy? You have inherited good genes and a healthy lifestyle from your family. Your family strengths and gifts need to be recognized as well as the limitations. Strengths and weaknesses are often linked in families.

Exercise: Identify and write down your family strengths. Identify and write down your family weaknesses.

If I had been an only child I probably would not be as socially adept as I am. Being one of eight children helped me learn to hold my own space, negotiate, compromise, and sense body language and emotions, long before others learned these skills.

Exercise: If you were an only child, how did you learn personal interaction and social skills outside of school? If you were a child with one or more siblings, how did you learn to deal with isolation and loneliness?

Remember, **we chose our birth family because we agreed in advance to deal with this particular karma in this lifetime.** We need to appreciate the gifts our family gave us in order to learn, grow and expand in this life. Struggle, hardship and pain define our character, and often lead us to self-discovery and Spirit.

What is Ancestral Lineage Clearing?

As you can tell from my earlier stories, **Ancestral Lineage Clearing is an advanced healing technique** through which people go back into an ancestor's historical past to change a dysfunctional pattern in their own life. By doing so, we can bring more health, wealth, joy, prosperity, better relationships and love into this present life. The facilitator basically asks the ancestor who set a negative precedent to aid the client in healing the issue leading from the ancestor's lifetime.

Family patterns are sometimes the most difficult to recognize because they are ingrained in us from such a young age. We can readily identify the larger inherited mental and emotional patterns. For example, Father was domineering; Mother was a wilting flower; you are an overachiever to satisfy your parents' dreams; an education is important; being married fulfills you; women should have children; etc.

 Exercise: Identify the major inherited mental and emotional dreams in your family and in your life.

I firmly believe many of our thoughts, beliefs, values, and attitudes come to us through generational lines that stretch back hundreds and thousands of years. These patterns become incorporated into our genetic material such as our DNA, which in turn influence the physical, emotional, mental and spiritual aspects of our lives.

In the cable TV show, *Who Am I,* the producers traced the genealogical history of celebrities. The program then showed how much the celebrity had in common with his or her ancestors. The celebrity inherited the looks and bone structure of the ancestors as well as many common personality traits such as ambition, showmanship and drive.

There are **many subtle family wounds.** They may go back many generations, and we do not generally recognize them as family patterns. These family wounds continue to appear and influence our lives today. The DNA that makes up our physical structure holds some of the same genetic coding passed down along generational lines. Some of this coding makes an effort to recreate patterns that cause us to subconsciously reenact the wounds of earlier generations, whether these wounds are physical, emotional, mental or spiritual.

When we recognize that these wounds do not belong in our lives and are willing to change them, we can dramatically improve our lives for the good. We become freer and happier when we can heal our anger, addiction, abuse, bad jobs, bad relationships, and mental and emotional challenges.

Some people can deal with their problems from a strictly personal point of view, such as, "I have a money issue. I cannot seem to hold onto money. I spend every cent I earn." Sometimes these issues are personal to that person. If their parents and other relatives carry the same issue, then it may be a generational challenge. If they perceive this attitude and behavior as their own, or only learned from their immediate parents, it may limit their ability to heal this challenge.

There may also be a **generational wound ingrained** over hundreds of years that needs to be addressed; otherwise, the subject matter will not be ultimately resolved. Ancestral family patterns can be inherited through multiple generations and **permutations of the original patterns can develop over the ages.** This also means subsequent generations are at risk.

Moreover, **each individual comes into this lifetime carrying his or her own agenda** of issues to clear. Each of us comes into this lifetime with projects and goals we want to accomplish from prior lives that may not be associated with the ancestors of our birth family. These can cause confusion about why we need to clear issues we *know* we have already dealt with before, but that continue to haunt us.

For example, many of the poverty and money issues arising today are a result of inheriting patterns from ancestors who were slaves and had no money. Other money issues arise from wealthy ancestors who spent money indiscriminately and had no conception of money management. Money issues may arise from negative religious concepts of wealth or money and may be reinforced during this lifetime by relatives.

This is the time to shift from the old paradigm to a new view of self, the world and the future. In order to transform we must heal the old wounds and open to the new energy of hope, happiness, love, health and joy.

Conclusion

When ancestral wounds negatively influence our present life, we have a tremendous opportunity to clear this pattern from our family lineage. *From a spiritual and energetic perspective, it means the time is ripe for this wound to be healed, and banished from our lineage and the planet.* **If you are feeling drawn to do this type of healing work for yourself or others, you have been selected to clear this challenge from your own family and perhaps others.**

Chapter III
The Basis of Ancestral Lineage Clearing

Why Heal Old Family Patterns?

What do we most want in life? Is it wealth, fame, love, power, immortality, genius, or to fly to the Moon?

No, **most of us just want to be happy!** The Dalai Lama, one of the most powerful Spiritual Leaders of the world today, gave us this simple message:

> *It is our basic right to be a happy person, happy family, and eventually a happy world. That should be our goal.*

I agree with the Dalai Lama. He forever talks of returning to our true essence of love, which is a joyful and happy state of being.

Happiness is an elusive concept for many people. Happiness means feeling good physically, having a positive mental outlook, doing fulfilling work, and both loving and being loved. These simple wishes are only accomplished by dedication to them within our complicated world. It really is easier than we think once we learn that **happiness comes from within our hearts** rather than from the outside world.

When we understand that **we can heal ourselves** we are on the road to healing all the ills of our life. There are many techniques and practices to help us learn how to heal ourselves from the inside out.

Reverend Misa Hopkins authored a book called *The Root of All Healing; 7 Steps to Healing Anything*, in which she discusses the basics behind healing. Her conclusion is obvious when you think about it; i.e., although there are many specialists for healing physical, mental, emotional or spiritual wounds, the basic principle remains the same: no one heals us; we heal ourselves.

There are times when intervention is necessary. Professional assistance in some circumstances is definitely required. Acute wounds or trauma such as a broken arm, an unexpected business loss, extreme depression or a crisis in faith should be addressed immediately. These are situations in which the support of our families and possibly a professional is suitable. Doctors, lawyers, ministers and other experienced persons can greatly aid us in times of crisis and stress. I would not try to set a broken arm on my own; I would call a doctor.

When challenges recur time after time in our lives they become chronic. Sometimes such issues are a result of personalities and behaviors developed during this lifetime. Often they develop as a result of family patterns from the wounds of the past.

Family wounds include childhood wounds, the wounds of our parents who influenced our environment, the wounds of our ancestors whose DNA coding we inherited and the wounds we inflicted upon ourselves and others. So how do we begin this journey to health, wealth and love?

We begin by healing our own bodies, minds, emotions and spirits. We can heal ourselves by learning what we need to know, going to school, taking classes, reading books, exercising, staying balanced, and surrounding ourselves with positive and supportive family and friends. It is also important to remember to seek and ask for help when we need additional support and assistance in our healing process.

If we are not healthy or strong enough physically to heal alone, we seek a health practitioner. If we are emotionally distressed we may seek counseling. If our physical, emotional or spiritual bodies are unbalanced and tangled up and we cannot seem to resolve patterns that have historical roots, choosing Ancestral Lineage Clearing will dramatically shift the energy in your life in a short period of time.

Why choose to ask our Ancestors to Help?

Our ancestors want to heal, and they want their children and future generations to heal. They are willing to help us become the best, healthiest, most prosperous, most loving and happiest people in the world.

In the Ancestral Lineage Clearing process we locate the primary ancestor with whom our present issue originated. This ancestor was unhappy with a choice or choices made in his or her life; otherwise, the health, prosperity, relationship, or spiritual challenge would not have been passed on to future generations in the family. These ancestors want their lives and the lives of their children changed for the better as much as you want yours altered for the better.

Just like most parents, **our ancestors are willing to change their lives** in order to make life better for themselves and their future descendants. If our ancestors – parents, grandparents, and great-grandparents – want us to be the best we can be, then why do we have these family challenges in our lives to begin with?

Decision-Making and Adversity

For example, at sixteen you fall in love for the first time. This person is the most beautiful, desirable, sexy, intelligent, funny and lovable person in the world. You *know* you would die if you ever lost this person. So, of course you want to marry him or her and live the rest of your lives together.

This is first love. It may last a week, a month, a year or forever. We do not have the information at sixteen to make such a momentous decision, even though we think we do, and we think that our feelings will never change.

Our parents know that first love may not be forever, and therefore generally do not permit their children to marry in that first rush of passion. Parents know that love changes, that people change and that life changes. Our decisions about a mate are very different at 16 than they are at 26 or even 36.

Exercise: Consider a decision you made multiple times in your life, perhaps in your 20s, 30s and 40s and so forth as you got older (such as buying a car). How did your decision (regarding what action to take) change over the years? Did your decision **process** *change over time (i.e. did you take into account* **different factors** *[change in color preference, fuel efficiency],* **more factors** *[include insurance costs, how many people the car would hold], did you make* **assumptions** *based on your prior decisions [like a particular brand that you decided to stick with instead of comparing makers])?*

Our ancestors made the best decisions they could make with the information they had at the time. How could they know their actions would impact future generations for hundreds or thousands of years later?

My sister Julie had a major heart attack at age 43. When she entered the hospital she was not expected to live. Julie was a healer and I knew she had been working on healing her wounded heart for many years.

I knew this heart condition came from the maternal side of the family. Our mother had a heart condition that began at age 27 and she ultimately died from it at age 76. Several members of my mother's family had heart conditions or died of heart attacks. The year before my sister's heart attack my brother had two stints put in his heart and the doctors discovered that he had had an undiagnosed heart attack ten years earlier.

Later, after Julie had recovered, I went into ceremony to do an Ancestral Lineage Clearing. As I began the Lineage Clearing journey this is what I saw:

Broken Heart

As I emerged from the time stream I was in Europe sometime prior to 1000 AD. I saw a warrior armed for battle settling his wife and children into their one room mud and straw home. He gave them orders to stay there until the fighting was over.

He knew their village was going to be attacked and the men were ready. They had all their weapons and the defenses planned. The women and children were in the safest places.
Afraid of the attackers, some villagers had already fled. He scorned such cowards. He was strong, and he would defend his home and village from all who sought to take what was theirs.

The raiders attacked with a huge force. The villagers were surprised at the number of the enemy. They had thought that only the adjacent village had sought to take their land, and it now appeared they had combined with others to overrun their homes.

The villagers fought long and hard. The warrior saw his friends and comrades slaughtered before his eyes, and the raiders began burning their homes. As he turned to scream at the women to run, he was struck in the head with a massive blow that knocked him unconscious.

He awoke hours later to the smell of blood, smoke and burning flesh. He gradually made it to his feet with a spinning head and a swirling stomach. He looked around. No one and nothing was moving.
He started wandering through the ruins. The dead were strewn about. The raiders had not taken anyone as slaves; they had killed everyone. Then it struck him—his wife, his children! He rushed home.

The house lay smoldering in ruins. Outside the door lay his wife with the babe in her arms, both dead. He grabbed a tree branch and shoved the bricks aside to find the remains of his other children, who had burned in the house. He didn't realize one son had escaped into the forest, hiding and in shock.

He screamed. They were his life. He lived for his family. All was gone. His brethren, his beloved, his sons, his daughters and his life . . . all were taken from him. Why hadn't he also died in battle as a warrior should?

As he knelt holding his beloved wife and child, he felt his heart break. He could not and would not take any more hurt and pain in this life. This was too much.

This emotional pain was too overwhelming to live with. He felt the massive pain in his heart squeeze the life from his body. He surrendered to the agony. It was no worse than the agony of his loss. He wanted to die, and so he did.

My ancestor's decision to die of a broken heart after losing his wife and children in a massacre was made from out of the depths of his grief. He thought he had nothing to live for, and did not know his choice to die of a broken heart would bring despair and heart disease into the family for generations to come.

The result of his decision altered the genetic pattern of his descendants without his knowledge. He never would have made such a decision if he had known what effect his choice would have on the lives of his remaining child and later generations.

I asked him on his death bed if he would like to change his life to make a difference. He grasped the opportunity to do so.

He went back to the day of the raid and chose to depart with those villagers who sought a new place to live without constant attack. They traveled for many weeks until they were far from the known territories of any other tribe.

They established a new village. The first few years were difficult. Many lives were lost to starvation and disasters until they settled in and began to build, strongly and safely. Thereafter, the village thrived.

He became the warrior chief and trained the young men to hunt and defend their territory from animals and strangers. He also taught them that violence was not a worthy way of life. Warriors were protectors, not destroyers.

He lived a long life, and saw his children live to marry and bear grandchildren. When he died, he was happy and fulfilled with his life.

This was the new energy I brought forward into the present. I incorporated this energy into my life and the lives of our family, knowing it would also encompass my sister in her current health crisis.

Julie recovered from her heart attack, although she had some complications afterward. Several months later I asked if she had made the decision to stay on earth at this time. She said that she had carefully considered whether it was time for her to cross over and decided she had too much left to do in this lifetime. Julie consciously made the choice to heal from the heart attack.

By performing the Ancestral Lineage Clearing the old energy pattern of running away from life's pain was now broken, and the new energy of choosing life was established. This enabled Julie to choose life during her crisis.

In Native American tradition **the elders consider the impact of their decisions to the**

seventh generation. That is, they consider the consequences their decisions will have on the great grandchildren of their grandchildren. If we all considered our decisions to the seventh generation, I believe we would take more time to make important choices in life.

We know that all life is interrelated. The so-called 'Butterfly Effect' of Chaos Theory says that the flap of the wings of a butterfly in Japan might have significant repercussions on wind strength and movements throughout the weather systems of the world, and theoretically could eventually, cause a hurricane in the Caribbean. In the same way, merely altering a single event in our own life has significant consequences in our future lives.

What if we had never gone to that party where we met the person we married? Might we perhaps not have divorced ten years later, unhappy, broke and unemployed? Maybe our life would have changed by meeting someone else or remaining single.

However, if we never made a mistake, we would never learn or grow. A child learns how to walk by trying a single step to find his balance. He falls, gets up and tries again. We learn how to drive by over-steering one way, then the other, until we get it right.

— **Adversity teaches us our strengths**, shows us where we need to grow and allows us to mature in ways we might not have done without the challenges that life presents. We all know overprotected and sheltered children who do not know how to manage their clothes, money, cars or jobs without someone taking care of them. I had a roommate once who called her father because her car wasn't working. Her father drove 300 miles to check on her car, only to discover it was out of gas.

When our ancestors overcame adversity in a positive way, they left positive skills in our genes that we take advantage of daily in order to be successful in our lives.

When adversity overwhelmed our ancestors, and their reactions resulted in life-damaging behaviors or belief systems, the consequences were unhappiness and negativity. If these patterns were not healed in subsequent years or generations they continued to be passed on; thus, undesirable family patterns were established.

These negative patterns were often established out of fear, loss, pride, or simply inadequate information about the significances of their decisions. If we all could see the results of our decisions ten to twenty years later, many of us would choose differently.

Every decision made, every day, has consequences we cannot foresee. There are multiple possible outcomes for each decision: positive, negative or neutral. Some consequences may be insignificant and some may be huge. Often, at the time of a decision, we have no way of knowing the resulting outcome.

We should not be afraid of making choices and decisions; they make us who we are today.

We can choose to be happy, healthy and loving individuals, with happy, healthy children.

When it comes to a major decision such as marriage, a move across town or across the country, a new job or career, a new relationship or a major family crisis, then we need to fully consider all the implications and consequences. Our choices impact not only ourselves but the lives of those around us, especially our family. Accept challenges and adversity with the spirit of adventure and opportunity. This is an opportunity for growth and learning.

The beauty of Ancestral Lineage Clearing is evident when we go back to an ancestor's life. Asking the ancestor to shift to the Choice Point and remake a momentous decision that will change his or her whole life is breathtaking. This decision has affected the lives of countless people in the future, and this ancestor is willing to take on this responsibility at your request.

In my ancestor's case of the warrior with the heart attack, his **Choice Point** was just prior to the invasion when he had the opportunity to take his family elsewhere, or to stay and fight. If he had taken them elsewhere, they would have lived, and heart dis-ease would not be a generational issue in my family. He had no way of knowing that at the time. When given the choice to take the family and live, he did not hesitate to choose life and happiness. He set aside his pride and selected an opportunity for growth even though it involved change.

If we are taught that our every decision truly makes a difference in our life, we can make more thoughtful choices at every stage of our life.

Conclusion

Our ancestors want to help us heal family wounds that they participated in creating. Although adversity can make us strong and contribute to our growth, sometimes we react inappropriately out of fear or pride and inadvertently cause disruptive family patterns to be passed on to following generations. This is an opportunity for our ancestors to help us clear those patterns.

Chapter IV
Theoretical Basis of Altering Family Patterns

Nature vs. Nurture

A debate has run for decades about whether or not our genetic patterns or our environments have more influence on our lives. Some scientists favor the view that genetics determines the outcome of our lives. Supposedly, our DNA coding establishes our personalities, physical attributes, attitudes and proclivities. Some psychologists, like B. F. Skinner, argue that despite our DNA, our upbringing and the values and attitudes we learn from our parents and other people in our formative years play a greater role in who we become as adults.

It has been known for a long time that certain dis-eases are family related either by genetics or by family environment. Genetic coding is just coming into its prime with the structure of DNA, having been relatively recently discovered in the 1950s by Linus Pauling. Scientists have since been hard at work identifying which genes control our bodily functions, including dis-eases.

A 60-year survey, the *National Survey of Health and Development*, conducted by the British government and run by the Medical Research Council, supports the latter view. The survey began in the 1950s, tracked 5,000 children born in 1946 every five years and concluded in 2007: "Children

43

who were born into better socioeconomic circumstances were most likely to do well in school and university, escape heart disease, stay slim, fit and mentally sharp and, so far at least, to survive." http://tiny.cc/britishsurveygenetics

The debate has lasted so long without a clear resolution because both genes and environment heavily influence who we are in the present. An interesting discussion of some of the contemporary issues appears in the public television series, Nova presentation, *Cracking the Code of Life.* http://tiny.cc/Nova-genomes. Of course, we can always break away from our early childhood training through intervention and help from the right sources.

Our DNA can determine our intelligence, height, the color of our eyes, hair and skin, and some propensities to genetically linked diseases, such as arthritis, heart dis-ease and other ailments. Just because our parents or grandparents had a genetically-linked dis-ease is no guarantee we will suffer from the same. Some dis-eases are behaviorally or environmentally linked, such as lung cancer from air pollution or smoking, radiation poisoning or cholera.

Only two of the eight children in my family appear to have inherited the heart problems that affected both our parents. The rest of us either did not inherit the gene or it is dormant. What caused my brother and one of my sisters to manifest this condition? I certainly do not have the answer at this point, nor can it be explained by science.

What we do have in common is family environment. Environment may not determine the color of your eyes in this generation, but it can affect your attitude towards, or about life. I was raised in a high stress environment in which my father smoked and drank. Both my brother and sister with the heart condition smoke, but then again, so do some of my other sisters. Why are only two affected?

Quite a bit of our personalities, habits and attitudes are developed early on, before we have any understanding of ourselves or of the world. Our 'world view' – our beliefs about ourselves, whether life is safe or people are trustworthy, the value of money, our work attitudes and our beliefs about marriage – are often subconsciously formed from the attitudes and models we receive from our parents.

Most psychologists say that it is not our conscious training or beliefs that create difficulties for us in the world; rather, it is the unspoken rules we learned that we nevertheless implicitly adopted. We learned these rules from family members, religious institutions, schools and teachers, and in our communities.

Furthermore, our love creates a subconscious as well as a conscious loyalty to our family's belief system and way of life. Of course, the way we were raised was *right* and other ways are *wrong* or *bad*, or perhaps just different. Families inherently protect their ways of life and their own ways of being.

Our attitudes about work, for example, can greatly affect our lives. Are work and career or family life and relationships more important? Do

45

bosses and managers use all their employees just to make a buck, or are they helping us to maximize our talents and serve the community? Do we have to work long and hard just to get by in life, or is work fun and fulfilling? Our world view affects our perception of every aspect of our life.

Kara's indecisiveness propelled her ancestral search. She didn't know what to do with her life, though she had a wide range of interests and talents, and therefore a wide range of possible choices for her life.

Indecisiveness

When Kara stepped out of the Time Stream she saw a man standing on the side of a forested green hill overlooking a sawmill by a river. He was in his 30's and the manager of this successful mill with many men under his command. Piles of finished logs, sheds of equipment, horses and carts were beside the sawmill. Along the river were buildings where the men lived, and where the cooking, laundry and everyday work of supporting a large task force was performed. Although he was proud of what he had done, he always had doubts and uncertainties about his capability.

Suddenly a piercing scream cut through the noise of the mill and of the men and horses outside. The great buzz saw inside the mill stopped and someone rushed out and yelled,

"Ezra got caught in'n the buzzer."

The manager stumbled down the hill and froze at the bottom, as men came pouring out of the mill shouting and yelling. Some stopped and asked him what to do, but he was stunned. His mind was a blank, and he cowered inside. He clearly did not know what to do. His assistant took one look at his chalk-white face and began issuing orders. They got Ezra out of the mill and put a tourniquet around the arm that had been sheared off. One man was sent into town for the doctor and the other men were ordered back to work outside the mill.

After everything had calmed down, the assistant brought his manager to the office and gave him a shot of whiskey. He didn't say anything; they both knew the manager was useless when the men were in a crisis. While he could handle the business, the equipment, direct the logging and deal with any technical problems, he just couldn't handle people.
Once the crisis had passed the manager quit. He could no longer take the stress. He moved to another city and took a job in a shop in which he had no responsibilities. He lived a quiet life in a boarding house without many friends. Marrying a quiet woman without passion and little feeling, they had two children. As a father, he loved his children distantly. When he died he felt discontented, unfulfilled, and ready to be released from this dismal life.

When Kara asked him to go to the **Choice Point** in his life, he went back to his childhood.

He was on the playground of a one-room schoolhouse. He watched as three bullies a chubby boy who was in tears, but they continued to poke and push him.

In his original life he had walked away, though he felt badly about abandoning the boy he knew. This time, he mustered up his courage, fisted his hands and walked over to the group. He shouted to the bullies,

"Stop that!"

They just laughed at him.

Again he shouted, "Stop that!"

"Why?" asked the biggest bully

"Because it's not right. He's not doing nothin' to you."

The bully replied, "Maybe we outta punch on you, then?"

"OK. At least I can punch back!"

He swallowed and braced himself for a beating. He didn't much like pain, but he could not stand by and watch them continue to pick on the chubby kid day after day.

The big bully said, "Well if'n you're going to fight back then it's no fun.

C'mon boys. Le's look som'where's else.

He was shocked that he wasn't going to be beaten into the dust. The chubby boy burst into a flood of tears and threw himself into his arms, sobbing his thanks. After that they became best friends. Later, when the manager went into the logging business, the chubby boy, who had grown into a big, strong muscular man, became his logging supervisor.

He grew up confident in making small decisions every day and in facing challenges. Ezra did fall into the saw and lose his arm, but the manager knew how to handle the situation and the men respected him and his judgment. He eventually ended up owning the mill and became a prosperous businessman in the community.

The manager married a young woman with whom he had fallen deeply in love and built her a fine house with lumber from the mill. They were both proud of their fine home and their two children, whom they loved deeply.

On his death bed, the manager was surrounded by his loved ones and mourned by the community. He felt he had lived a full, loving and useful life. He had chosen well in this lifetime.

The issue about indecision is to do what feels right in your heart even if the choice is challenging. Kara learned this from the session: she will always know the right choice if she will only stop and listen to her heart, even if the choice *seems* difficult. The first time is always the hardest, but becomes easier every time you make a decision.

Exercise: Consider in what areas of your life—financial, health, relationships and spiritual—environment or genetics was more influential.

World View

In the United States we share a common world view, and we take certain assumptions for granted. For example, we assume that the world is round, that atoms and molecules make up matter in the world, that we all die, that cars are driven on the streets, that planes fly in the air, that electricity makes electrical gadgets work, that water comes out of a faucet, that people live in houses, that we buy food in the grocery store, that we work to earn money, and that we can go to school. This may not be true for everyone, but it is true for most.

These are assumptions we absorb from our environment. If our parents and the people around us treated cars, planes and electricity as magical instruments, so would we. If doctors were considered priests with special gifts from the gods, we would hold that belief, too. People in other cultures honor their ancestors because they believe their ancestor can intercede for them with religious deities for special favors, or that they can cause harm through anger or neglect.

Some of these unconscious world views hamper us when we grow up. I know how uncomfortable I felt when I began making more money than my father. Although by that time I had not lived in the family home for ten years, I still had feelings of guilt. After all, my father was the head of the family and I was still his daughter.

I also felt uncomfortable when I bought my first home as a single woman in the 1970's. Single women did not own homes; home ownership was for families. Hence, another world view was shattered.

Husbands who stay home to parent young children while their wives go to work are shattering another American "ideal." This is wonderful for the terrific fathers who do a great parenting job. The first man to stay at home challenged this world view and family pattern. He most certainly received criticism and objections from his family for taking such an un-masculine role.

Our world view presents unconscious expectations that limit us. We can break these expectations to achieve feeling better about ourselves, our choices and our lives, if we can escape the confines of the acceptable world view. Change begins with the courageous, and people have always gone against the norm in order to create change.

Ancestral Lineage Clearing challenges our typical world view of time and space, the ability of our ancestors to aid us, and our ability to alter family patterns that affect future generations. This is a positive change for the Western World to adopt. Many people can energetically shift dysfunctional family patterns that now result in unhappiness, poverty, ill health and broken relationships in a very limited time, and without years of therapy.

Scientific World Views

In describing Ancestral Lineage Clearing, I was once asked for the scientific basis for claiming that it altered the DNA and shifted the energy pattern of the whole family around family patterns. However, **this energy technique is not based on a scientific or medical study.**

Since I have some scientific background, my left brain sought the answer to 'why' as well as 'how.' **This is my personal theory** based upon my layperson's understanding of Quantum Mechanics Theory. I have little understanding of the math behind the physics, and frankly I do not want to learn the advanced math necessary for this now.

My Theory

Ancestral Lineage Clearing is consistent with our presently acceptable scientific world view of relativity and Quantum Mechanics Theory as I understand it.

When our ancestor chose a certain energy pattern in his or her life with such emotional force, it set in motion a cellular change in his or her body that caused genetic changes to take place in the atoms and molecular structure of the body. These changes resonate with his/her children and are passed on, or affect their cellular structure.

So, how do we change the ancestor's past life and alter the DNA and the present?

Time: the present can influence the past and the future

Einstein theories at the beginning of the twentieth century revolutionized physics and particularly our notions of time. His theories of time and space have had scientists working to explain and expand his notions for the past century. Einstein's final words about time in 1955 were, "...the distinction of past, present and future is only a stubbornly persistent illusion . . ."

(For a general layperson's discussion of Einstein's theories of time, Kip Thorne's book, *Black Holes and Time Warps: Einstein's Outrageous Legacy* is a good place to begin.) Our general concept of **time is of the duration of time,** such as a minute, an hour, a day etc., progressing in a linear fashion. However, when I discuss time in connection with Ancestral Lineage Clearing, I am talking about time in terms of past, present and future.

Einstein's theory has been greatly discussed and abused by Stephen Hawking and Richard Feyman; however, new physicists have reinforced Einstein's original theory that time is an objective reality and that the future can influence the past. So, according to Einstein and present physicists, when we go back in time from the present to our ancestor's past, we can indeed influence the past. I recommend beginning with *Time's Arrow and Archimedes' Point,* by Huw Price, for a layman's discussion of Einstein's time theory. (For Stephen Hawking's derivation from Einstein's theory, read *A Briefer*

History of Time, by Stephen Hawking and Leonard Mlodinow.

Therefore, if the past is not linear, and if past, present and future are illusions, how can we think about time? If we consider time as a loop or circle, and the loop is malleable, then we can cross the time line from one point to another almost anywhere.

For example, think of all time as a rubber band (a loop), and imagine that we are standing at one point (call it point A) on the rubber band. Take the rubber band and twist it once.

, When we twist the rubber band, the place where we are standing (A) touches another point (B). We can see, hear, feel and touch the time from our present point on the rubber band (A) to any other point (past or present) that the loop touches on the rubber band, in this case point B. Theoretically, we can influence point B. Depending on how stiff the rubber band is, it is often easier to twist a loop in the middle of the rubber band (the farther past) than it is to twist a loop at the end (the near past; i.e., five years ago, for example). I think that is why it is more difficult to see into our own direct past than further into the past.

In Ancestral Lineage Clearing we move along the time loop to another point in time so that we can influence what happens in that past time. Although it may be possible to affect the future, not many people have dared to try.

Probability

All of us have numerous options, called probabilities, for making decisions in every moment of our lives. We do not necessarily think of them as alternate probabilities in that way. Otherwise we would probably go mad without constantly and automatically making small everyday decisions.

For instance, if I am standing on a street corner at a four way stop, I have more than four options: I can really go in a 360° direction. What step I take in any direction will choose the outcome of where I go, what I do and perhaps how my day goes.

Maybe if I cross the street on the diagonal, I will be hit by a car. If I go straight, I will go to work and make it on time. If I make it on time and get a good mark for promptness on my next evaluation, I will get a raise. If I detour to the bakery and buy doughnuts, I might be late and get fired.

The concept of probability is important in the Ancestral Lineage Clearing process since we will ask our ancestor to choose a point in his/her life in which to make a different decision that will change his or her life path. This *Choice Point* is a pivotal point in the past life for which the ancestor chooses an alternate reality and begins to live in the new reality, changing the energy of his/her lifetime. We will ask the ancestor to **choose another probability line** among all the possible probabilities s/he could have chosen at a particular time. **This is a critical element** in clearing the negative energy in a family pattern.

Quantum Mechanics

There are several theories of Quantum Mechanics that play into Ancestral Lineage Clearing.

According to quantum theory, waves and particles make up the essential elements called quantum particles in all atoms. Quantum matter can be either waves or particles at any given time, and can shift between waves and particles at will. These quantum particles and waves surround us, responding to our subconscious desires and intentions.

There are three theories I consider applicable to this healing modality:

1. An observer changes the outcome of the experiment observed.

2. When a related particle is changed, all other related particles are altered in the same manner, regardless of time and place.

3. The result of a hypothesis has a solution once the observers agree upon an outcome, when the observers do not know the outcome before they begin an experiment.

Quantum theory (in a very generalized way) states that we draw to us that which we truly desire and which reinforces our belief systems.

The first theory on the variability of an experiment's outcome based upon an observation made Quantum Mechanics hit the public headlines as well as the scientific journals. In the prior scientific world view, every experiment had a logical, reasonable, **permanent** solution that was replicable by any other scientist. When those physicists experimenting with quantum mechanics discovered that a different solution to a problem depended upon who was observing the experiment, it shook the scientific world.

It has now been well established in the physics community that this quantum theory is indeed true in the quantum world. It is not applicable in the larger physical world. This proposition is where the spiritual world formed the statement and belief that "we create our own reality." If we are the observers of our own lives, then it also follows that we control the outcome of our lives.

In the previous example, if I want to die (consciously or subconsciously), I will, also consciously or subconsciously, cut across the street diagonally and be hit by the car. If I want to do well at work I will choose to walk directly across the street and be at work on time. If I hate my job and truly wish to get away from it, I'll go to the bakery and get fired, thereby reinforcing my belief system that my bosses are out to get me. Our quantum particles will influence the outcome of our actions in order to produce our desired result.

If my belief system says that I will die of a broken heart if life gets too difficult, then I will draw quantum particles that will stimulate the atoms and molecules in my DNA **genetic coding** for heart disease. Further, if my **environment and early upbringing reinforces the belief that I will die of**

heart dis-ease, then more quantum particles will activate the DNA coding to make the chromosomes active instead of dormant. If I ignore my heart health by drinking, smoking and eating unhealthily, I will perpetuate heart dis-ease in the family. *(The Spontaneous Healing of Belief*, Greg Braden; *The Self-Aware Universe*, Amit Goswami, Ph.D., with Richard E. Reed and Maggie Goswami)

On the other hand, if I clear heart dis-ease energy through Ancestral Lineage Clearing, I will no longer draw quantum particles to myself or to my family. The belief system that draws the quantum particles to the atoms and molecules of the DNA coding for heart dis-ease has been altered and I do not, or no longer, draw these types of particles into my reality. My mental, emotional and spiritual focus is no longer a magnet for the quantum waves and particles of the configuration for heart dis-ease in my chromosomes and cellular material. **Every cell in my body reproduces itself every seven years, so that within seven years these cells will be replaced.**

If there is no attraction for the heart dis-ease coding, then these atoms and molecules will no longer be drawn to my body, the bodies of the children I influence, or to their children. **This genetic change is then passed on to future generations** through the new DNA and through the environment of the family belief system.

The second theory answers the most insistent questions about Ancestral Lineage Clearing. **How can this affect relatives that are not in our**

proximity or with whom we do not keep in contact?

There have been multiple long-distance experiments with quantum particles. These experiments have shown that when related particles are separated by thousands of miles (for example, one in a particle accelerator in Texas, the other in a particle accelerator in Switzerland), and **scientists change the spin on one particle from positive to negative, the other connected particle automatically and simultaneously changed.** (*Fabric of the Cosmos*, Brian Greene; *The Elegant Universe*, Brian Greene.)

To me, this answers the question of why the family members with the same genetic background can be affected by the change in the client's energetic field during an Ancestral Lineage Clearing session. **The client's quantum field is altered; therefore, any related quantum field is automatically changed, too.**

Initially, any change we make is on an energetic level. It can be felt in the client's body, emotions and spirit, but physically the DNA will not be altered immediately. With the resetting process of the client's energy field, the related energy fields are also changed. Once the changes move from the energetic field into physical form, we see physical change occur.

In the third theory, scientists studied other scientists who were conducting experiments. Those who studied the other scientists during the experiments discovered that a specific outcome of an unknown experiment was reached only when the experimenting group reached a consensus concerning what the result should be.

For example, let's say we set a pot of water to boil and set a timer to go off in five minutes. We want to find out when the water reaches boiling temperature, but we then leave the room without knowing how long it will take to boil. The timer goes off in five minutes, and when we check the water in the pot it is boiling. We conclude that it takes five minutes for the water to boil.

Then, three of us decide to determine how long it will take the same pot to boil when we watch it. So we set a timer to go off when it is triggered by the boiling temperature. We stand around watching the pot get hot. One of us says, "I think it will boil in three minutes." Another says, "No, it will take at least ten minutes to boil." The third says, "I think it will take five minutes."

We all watch as the water heats. As it gets closer to boiling it becomes clear that it will take longer than three minutes to boil, but fewer than ten minutes. At some point all three of us look at the water and the time, and agree that it will take six minutes for the water to boil. **The water will then actually boil in six minutes**.

The implication of this result is that a group consciousness can influence the outcome of actions or events. For example, if a council gathers for a peace conference to settle a violent conflict and the people attending the conference **do not want peace, or do not believe that peace is possible or**

probable, the peace conference will fail. If we as a people do not fully believe humanity can live in peace, we will never see peace.

Our beliefs and agreements create the results we seek. These belief systems are our boxes – our picture frames of life. If we cannot see outside our boxes or outside the frames that border our lives, then our lives cannot change. This is why advisors favor telling us to "think outside the box."

Remember, these statements are not scientifically proven. This is only **my theory of how Ancestral Lineage Clearing works, based upon my understanding of quantum theory.** As a lay person I cannot prove this theory.

Hopefully, the scientific community will have enough interest one day in the future to undertake a study of time, quantum theory, ancestral healing and other healing techniques, to verify if my theory is correct. You can decide for yourself whether you feel my theory is correct, or just try Ancestral Lineage Clearing and see if it works for you. Many people have found it works for them without any theoretical basis at all.

Conclusion

Healing our family patterns through Ancestral Lineage Clearing is a way to better health, wealth, love and happiness in our own lives. With the help of our ancestors we can change the environmental and genetic patterns that have a negative impact on our lives and the lives of our children.

For those of us who need a logical understanding of why this healing modality works, Ancestral Lineage Clearing is consistent with Einstein's principles of moving through time, and the quantum theory that we create our own reality through our conscious and unconscious desires. These are my personal theories as to why Ancestral Lineage Clearing functions so well, although no scientific tests in this field have been conducted to date.

Chapter V
Changing Family Patterns

Affecting Family Wound Patterns

Healing negative family patterns is an **energy healing technique**. It is similar to healing prayers, energy balancing, Reiki energy work, quantum touch, soul retrieval, Hellinger family constellation work, various psychological methods for dealing with family trauma, and non-medical, spiritual counseling. By altering energetic patterns in the family history, negative energy patterns are positively affected.

Even though all energy fields are intertwined and cannot truly be separated, for teaching and healing purposes it is sometimes helpful to approach energy fields as though they are separate. There are several systems for exploring the energy fields of the body.

Many spiritual communities teach that every person has **four energy bodies: 1. Physical, 2. Emotional, 3. Mental and 4. Spiritual (PEMS).** Each body has an energy field associated with it.

1. The **physical body** is readily seen, felt, smelled and heard. An observer can usually tell if a body is healthy by noticing the color of the skin, the odor, the vitality of the person, the sound of the voice and the overall appearance. At times, medical tests are necessary in order to diagnose the preliminary stages of a dis-ease of the body.

As the previous story of the heart dis-ease in the earlier chapter demonstrates clearing ancestral patterns in the body can shift physical illnesses in the present.

Warning: Do Not Stop taking medication or seeing your health care practitioner even after the ancestral energy has been cleared.

Exercise: Review your history of physical health and compare it to family patterns of dis-ease in both the maternal and paternal sides of your family. Be sure to consider your grandparents, children, siblings (brothers and sisters), aunts, uncles and cousins.

Although the energy has been cleared, our physical bodies need time to adjust to the new energy. Our bodies have probably been living with a dis-ease for many years, and will need to heal on the physical level with the support of medication, supplements and treatments, until they can learn to function independently. We will find it easier to heal and to move through the stages of the dis-ease as we progress.

Even after the Ancestral Lineage Clearing and my sister's recovery from the first heart attack, she remained on medication. She had a second heart attack about a year later because the doctors could not stabilize her heart medication. When healing from old wounds, **it is critical that professional assistance and advice are followed**.

Exercise: Prepare yourself in a meditative state and scan your body – gently starting at the top of your head and reviewing every organ and muscle in your body, and sense, feel, hear or visualize – noticing if there is any tension, darkness, smokiness, chaos, redness or indication that something is not right, wholesome, healthy or in order. Practice this exercise until you can go deeply into the affected organ, into the cells and perhaps into the atoms. Follow your intuition and any directions you get from your body for any healing you may need.

2. A keen observer notices the **emotional health** of a person through appearance and behavior. For example if we are happy, we pay attention to our appearance and cleanliness, have a good **energy** level for our age and health, we are interesting or interested in work and relationships, and are active participants in life.

Many issues fall within this category. My family has a history of generational sexual abuse that only became known within our family during the past 15 years. Sexual abuse is very traumatic and takes a huge emotional toll on everyone in the family, even if not all family members are involved. A more complete discussion of this issue can be found in Chapter I. I used the Ancestral Lineage Clearing method to alter this negative family pattern from our family lineage when I was just beginning to learn how to use this clearing process.

Once I cleared the sexual and physical abuse on my mother's side it was easier for me to release my abuse and trust issues with men. Then, after healing this pattern on my mother's side of the family I did a lineage clearing around sexual abuse on my father's side of the family. This resulted in a major emotional shift in my life and in the lives of other family members. This work allowed my other sisters to face some of their family abuse issues.

Issues such as depression, anxiety, grief, frustration, lack of direction, hopelessness and generalized malaise may all be the product of familial situations. Once crucial medical conditions are eliminated and family history is considered, many adverse emotional subjects can be addressed by this method of healing.

3. Mental Health is sometimes obvious for observers too. A healthy person is alert, aware of his or her surroundings, and capable of daily tasks such as handling money, a job, happy and healthy relationships, driving a car, grocery shopping and living a *normal* life. Persons with mental challenges may find it difficult to follow conversations, may become confused when more than one person is talking and may be unable to make sensible financial decisions or take adequate care of themselves. For some this disability is genetic; for others it is a matter of dis-ease, stress or mental health condition.

Sometimes it is difficult to differentiate between emotional and mental health. In many cases the **definitions of emotional and mental health overlap**. Mental health relates to illness of the mind. Emotional health rests on the state of feelings. Is depression an emotional or a mental condition? Is happiness emotional or mental? From my perspective, the Western medical community considers any disorder that needs intervention to be mental health dis-ease.

I had a middle-aged client, Peter, who came to me because he had had severe chronic depression from the time he was a teenager. Apparently, his mother, father and several siblings also suffered from chronic depression. After consulting with him we thought it best, based on his family history, to do two separate generational clearings: one on the maternal side and one on the paternal side.

Depression

Father's Family Pattern

A man is being tortured in the dungeon of a castle in medieval times. He is hanging by his wrists and being burned with a red-hot poker as he is questioned about harboring a thief in the guise of a pilgrim who had stolen precious items from the castle several days before. The man is a farmer/shepherd/ serf who lives in a thatched hut on a hillside near the castle with his wife and child.

Four days ago at sunset, a stranger in pilgrim's garb came by, asking for food and a place to sleep. The man gave him dinner and shelter for the night.

As the story unfolds, the farmer's name is Mannlin. He was tending his fields the day the pilgrim came to his home. The stranger didn't look or act like a pilgrim; he wasn't humble, nor did he seem desperate for food. Most pilgrims didn't beg from farms or homes since they were welcome to food and lodging at churches and monasteries along the well-traveled pilgrimage trails.

Mannlin's farm was out of the way for a pilgrim on the road to any sacred shrine unless he was lost. Although he was hesitant, Mannlin didn't ask questions, but invited the stranger in to share the remnants of mutton stew and ale, and offered him a place by the hearth. Mannlin still felt uneasy and slept on a pallet next to the firewood with his knife at hand. When he awoke in the morning the pilgrim was gone.
A few days later the Lord's men came to him, inquiring about strangers. When he told them about the stranger they took him away to the castle and threw him in the dungeon. The soldiers didn't believe him when he couldn't answer the questions, and so the torture began. After they were finished, they threw him out on the streets, permanently crippled and scarred.

Mannlin went back to his hut and farm. He was continually depressed and periodically drank heavily. What had he done wrong, to deserve this punishment from man and God?

He remained bitter, aloof and angry, and, as a result of his attitude, he never really made friends nor was he close with his family. His children fled home as soon as they were old enough. His wife barely tolerated him. He died alone and unhappy.

Mother's Family Pattern

Ahentra was young, beautiful, spoiled and demanding. As the only child of a rich noble lord and lady of the capital city, she had been indulged since her birth by her parents, grandparents, the household slaves and everyone around her. Her beauty, charm and intelligence got her most of what she wanted; her tantrums got her the rest. By the time she reached marriageable age, her parents desperately prayed to find a suitable husband who could control her.

When her father suggested it was time for her to marry, Ahentra decided the only man good enough for her was the King. Her father was astonished at such a proposal. The King already had 20 wives; what did he need with another? Why did she want to marry the King?

Her father tried to change her mind, but she was adamant. She would marry the King and no one else.

Her father finally agreed to approach the king. When the King received the proposal, he was not particularly interested in another wife; however, he was interested in the proposed dower.

The wedding took place, and Ahentra was ecstatic. She had everything she ever wanted. Now she was Queen, and the King was her husband.

Her life as Queen was not as she expected, as she discovered she was just one of many in the harem and had no particularly great or unique status. She was not allowed to leave the palace or even the women's quarters. The King would come to her at night, but he never stayed the entire night.

She was excited when she became pregnant immediately. However, the only thing that changed was that she was coddled, cared for and stifled as the potential mother of a son of a King.

Ahentra was a strong, healthy young woman, and the pregnancy went well. She felt fine and lorded over everyone as a Queen–Mother. Nine months later, however, disaster struck. She gave birth to a girl-child! The King only had 6 sons, and he had 12 daughters. He didn't need another daughter.

Over the next three years she was called for by the King three times on the anniversary of their daughter's birth. She did not conceive on any of these occasions, and the King never called for her again.

She lived with the King's other wives, with no other purpose in life than the desperate hope and expectation of an invitation to join the King at night, and to bear a son.

Her daughter was raised with the King's children, though Ahentra saw her infrequently. As a political pawn, she was married to a distant king in a foreign land at the age of eight to seal an alliance, and Ahentra never saw her child again.

Ahentra had fulfilled her girlhood dream of becoming a Queen, but she was unloved; she loved no one, and no one cared about her. As a virtual prisoner in the King's harem, she had no purpose in life. She became more and more depressed over the years and, with no reason to live, Ahentra died a young woman.

We cleared the negative energy from both of these lifetimes. Peter recognized that these ancestors had felt hopeless and helpless because of the decisions they had made in their lives. He knew that in this lifetime, he now had the power to make choices that would allow him to have control over his own career, relationships and happiness.

After the second Ancestral Lineage Clearing session had cleared the depression pattern from both family backgrounds, Peter said he felt like a huge weight had been lifted off his shoulders. His depression was gone. He felt as if the chronic depression pattern that had plagued him all his life was now banished.

4. **Spiritual health** (often, but not necessarily equated with religion) is often more difficult to observe. Most people are hesitant to speak of their spiritual lives, except with family members or very close friends. If a person is faced with a crisis of faith, difficulty with an aspect of dogma, or a longing for closer relationship with the Divine, many times

only their spiritual counselor or partner may know about it.

Spiritual health pervades the essence of every person's life. Loss of spiritual health may manifest as a sense of hopelessness, lack of direction, inability to love or meaninglessness in life. Spiritual ill health sometimes manifests as the unexplained welling of volatile emotions like anger and frustration, or an obsessive drive for wealth, power or fame, without an underlying life purpose or with an enduring sense of futility. Since these emotions may also mask or combine with emotional or mental challenges, it may be difficult to separate the spiritual dilemma. **Without an underlying spiritual foundation most people cannot find a vital center to their lives to sustain them in times of crises.**

When most people speak of reading auras or energy patterns, they are generally seeing or *reading* a combination of all of the energy bodies surrounding a person.

How Energy Patterns Clear

Some master healers and eastern avatars actually physically see all four energy bodies – Physical, Emotional, Mental and Spiritual (PEMS) – as colors. They understand that **dis-ease first begins in the spiritual body, progressing first to the mental body and then to the emotional body before it reaches the stage of physical illness.** Therefore, we must recognize that we also heal from the spiritual energy level through the mental and emotional bodies before the physical body is healed.

If you think about the last time you caught a cold or got the flu, do you remember how you first started feeling fuzzy in the head and couldn't quite think straight? Perhaps you then became cranky (if you don't remember, ask you partner or co-workers! Then, your nose started running, you began sneezing, your stomach became upset, etc.

I have known people with cancer and those who have had heart attacks. They had not felt *quite right* for months before the actual physical symptoms showed up, and they began slipping mentally, forgetting small things like dates, appointments, birthdays, or picking up laundry. Their energy waned, and they were depressed or uninterested in their usual activities. They would say nothing was wrong, but something was definitely moving into their physical energy systems. If someone could have seen into these people's energy fields, they might have anticipated dis-ease showing up in these bodies.

About a year before my sister Julie's first heart attack, I was sitting at my kitchen table looking at a family picture, and I thought, "Julie's going to die." In that picture, her face was fuzzy and her energy was cloudy. I knew she was sick. Yet, she said she felt fine. She looked great, her physical energy was good, she was happy and everything "appeared" fine. About a year later, she almost died from her first heart attack before she reached the hospital. Her heart condition had not previously shown up physically, but it had appeared in her energy field.

These energy patterns can appear in families too. Physical illnesses that repeat throughout generations can be environmental as well as genetic. Heart dis-ease might be a result of bad diet, poor exercise, smoking, alcohol, stress, lack of belief in yourself, others and the Divine, emotional trauma and genetic material. All PEMS energy fields are affected.

When family patterns are cleared, the cleansing reaches all fields—the physical, emotional, mental and spiritual (PEMS) energy bodies. As the energy is purified at the point of origin in the ancestor's time, it clears immediately. The physical gene or genes that are associated with the dis-ease clears in this present generation may take as long as seven years to clear, if they are not cleared simultaneously.

In my family, when I cleared the heart dis-ease from my ancestor's life, Julie could heal her heart dis-ease in her life. She is now better and her heart is healing. Her last checkup showed that all was stable and her heart was strong.

Analyzing the Healing Process in Ancestral Lineage Clearing

When a client comes for a clearing session it is helpful to know if the family pattern to be healed is on the Physical, Emotional, Mental or Spiritual plane. The client may take longer to fully and completely heal if the healing is on the physical level since the energy must move through all the other energetic bodies first. This is why it is so important for medical and health assistance to be continued.

If the clearing takes place on the emotional or mental level the energetic clearing and resetting will be more rapid. Once you understand how the energetic system works and how to apply it to yourself and to your clients, it will be helpful in analyzing how the energetics are cleared and the patterns reset.

Conclusion

Many spiritual healing systems believe we have four energy bodies associated with our bodies: the Physical, Emotional, Mental and Spiritual (PEMS). When we begin to be ill, the dis-ease manifests first in the spiritual energy body, then in the mental energy body, the emotional energy body, and finally in the physical body. We then heal our bodies in the reverse order; physically, emotionally, mentally, and finally spiritually.

If we analyze the client's healing challenge and know on which energetic level the healing needs to take place in the family pattern, it will be simpler to release the energy from that particular energetic field and reset the energy in the correct field for healing. The other energetic fields will then naturally follow the healing progression.

Chapter VI
Specific Family Patterns and Common Questions

Why Me?

According to many spiritual masters we choose our family and life before we are born or incarnated onto Earth. When we are still spirits, we decide whom our parents and siblings will be, whom we will meet and what lessons we will face in this particular lifetime.

Even though we choose to be born into a specific family with siblings, and aunts, uncles, cousins and other relatives, each person experiences this life in a unique way and brings his or her own past life experiences with them. Many clients ask why they are affected by a particular family pattern and others are not. Why do **these clients** have to deal with poverty, abuse, mental illness, cancer, depression, relationship issues, etc.:

Because we are the ones most capable of resolving and clearing this pattern in our lifetimes. Other relatives have different challenges that they will have an opportunity to resolve.

We make a contract with our own higher spirit about the challenges this lifetime will encompass. Many people believe we choose the same family groupings over and over in different lifetimes to work out relationship issues, because of our endearing and enduring love for each other.

We are here to support our families in their growth, as they are here to support our growth. Even if we are estranged from some of our family, or have difficulty accepting their life styles or behavior patterns, those family members are a part of our development, environment, choices, values, relationships and worldview. They may be supporting us by being a difficult part of the life we choose. This choice affects who and what we are and the challenges we face.

Childhood challenges are our greatest blessings. They come to us at a vulnerable age and we are often greatly wounded by them. However, they also give us strength and the power to overcome great difficulties later in life. We have many years left in our lives to overcome early childhood obstacles that we may not have been able to overcome had they occurred later in life.

In addition to our **biological families** or the families we grew up with, we all tend to gather our **spiritual families** at some point in life. These are the friends of the heart and soul who sustain us, carry us through hard times, lead us into developing our higher selves and bring out the best in us. They may be our spouses, partners, best friends, teachers, or sometimes people who drop into our lives for a short while to guide us to the next level of spiritual development. We always give ourselves friends to help us through the challenges in this life if we are open to recognizing them.

Not everyone in the family is alike

Certain patterns manifest in some family members from the maternal side and others manifest from the paternal side of the family. Sometimes these patterns overlap from both sides of the family in one or more family members. It is rare for all family members to show identical inherited patterns. In many cases certain patterns will skip a generation, such as is often true in alcoholism, for example. That is why it is important to look at the entire genealogical history when searching for family patterns.

Additionally, every individual is unique. We are born into this world with a diversity of experiences from past lives, pregnancy and birthing experiences, parents, grandparents, relatives, early and later childhood involvements, birth order, food and environmental influences, education and personality traits. All of these influences are filtered by each individual.

Everything and everyone we encounter influences who and what we are. We are different from our parents and siblings – even a twin sibling. The specific effect of a single gene or set of genes on an individual is still unknown.

We all see this every time we look at our families. No one looks or behaves exactly alike. There is Uncle Joe, the family comedian who keeps everyone laughing and never lets anyone close. Or, Aunt Mary, who is always in the kitchen making sure everyone is fed, and then cleaning up. You can never get her to socialize unless you're in the kitchen with her. Then there is John, the gossip, who has to know everything everyone else is doing. Suzie is the quiet one. She never says much, but she observes and listens to peoples' hearts.

In addition to personalities, everyone has their own challenges even if we do not see them. Do not assume someone in the family has escaped the family *curse*. They may merely hide it better than you.

Adoption Issues
Biological Family

The question often arises whether Ancestral lineage Clearing works if you are adopted and do not know your birth parents. Of course it does! Ancestral Lineage Clearing follows your ancestors on an energetic level. **You do not need to have any knowledge of your biological parents at all.**

Although environment affects our outlook, values and lifestyle, many of our attributes are established by our genetic make-up and the family patterns contained therein. If you have challenges that you cannot particularly pinpoint as originating from your adoptive parents, your environment or education, then such challenges may very well be linked to an ancestral pattern.

There have been many studies of twins adopted by separate families who have married spouses of the same name and nature, hold the same type of job, and have similar health issues, hobbies and lifestyles. These features generally arise from genetic inclinations.

If you look at the challenges in your life that are not associated with your environment, they are most likely derived from unknown family patterns. These family patterns will reveal themselves when you search for the core issue and use your intuition to *feel* whether the challenge is from the maternal or paternal side of the family. This may seem difficult to determine from reading this book, but once you begin the process it tends to flow easily and smoothly. Remember, your ancestors **want** to help you.

When you begin to search for the original ancestor who initiated the issue, he or she will definitely appear. They will be waiting for you.

Adoptive or Foster Family

Whether you know your birth family or not, and for some reason you were later placed in an adoptive or foster family, in some ways you have access to additional resources. **Both your birth family and the family who raised you, and their ancestors, have agreed on an energetic level to assist you on your journey in this lifetime.**

You have been influenced by placement in their environment and by how you were raised by them. You have absorbed their values, attitudes, lifestyles and worldviews. They, too, want you to succeed and be happy. Their ancestors can assist you in healing wounds arising from childhood incidents, influences and environmental conditions that do not necessarily reside in the DNA coding. At times it may be the foster/adoptive family's ancestor who will aid you in resolving the issue at hand.

Be open to assistance from your adoptive or foster family ancestors. Help is all around us if only we are courageous enough to ask.

Children's Participation

I do not recommend that children take part in Ancestral Lineage Clearing. Neither their brains nor their bodies are developed enough to maintain the concentration necessary to meditate or hold the energy of making a journey to find an ancestor. Although a parent can determine a child's issue, the child cannot actively participate in a session.

Having said the above, a parent can hold the energy and participate in an Ancestral Lineage Clearing session on behalf of a child. **Generally, a parent would do an Ancestral Lineage Clearing for him or herself and clear the issue that is disturbing the child. By clearing the issue in the parent, the issue would clear in the child.**

However, **if you have adopted a small child**, have a long-term foster child or are raising a child left in your care that may have an issue unrelated to your side of the family(such as a grandchild), it may be suitable to the child's benefit.

A client-mother heard of Ancestral Lineage Clearing from a friend and discussed with me whether it would help her seven-year-old adopted Chinese daughter. Her daughter had been abandoned when she was 18 months old, in the snow, in front of an orphanage, apparently because of her severe cleft palate.

This young girl was troubled with sleep difficulties, and felt worthless and undeserving. She could not make friends and she avoided going out in public, even though her cleft palate had been repaired. She did not want to go for walks with her mother and sister, even for exercise, and was depressed.

I had never done a third-party Ancestral Lineage Clearing, though I was certainly willing to try. This little girl clearly needed help.

I met with her adoptive mother and we set the intention to find the original ancestor who began the abandonment issue in her family and participate in an Ancestral Lineage Clearing session for her adopted daughter.

The Baby-Killers

The Matriarch was dressed in black and sat in a large ornate chair in the dimly lit room. The windows were shaded with intricately carved wooden screens that kept intrusive eyes from prying.

The newborn was brought in by one of the midwives. The Matriarch inspected the naked child. The baby was healthy and its cry lusty. Another son for the clan, "Good." she thought. She turned the child over and a shiver of horror quickly ran through her as she saw a huge strawberry-colored birth mark on the back of his head. Of course it would not show when his hair grew out, but when he bred, one of his children might have a birth mark on its face.

This will not do. The clan children must be perfect. No blemish or flaw must be permitted to infect the bloodline. It was an honor to be a member of this clan in the land that would later be called China.

The Matriarch called the guard. "Take him away." The guard silently removed the baby to dispose of him without fuss. This was the job of the guards of the Women's palace. The Matriarch's Word was Law. If the guard disobeyed, he was beheaded.

A young, beautiful girl lived in the Women's Palace along with all the other young women. This particular young woman was being groomed for special treatment since she showed exceptional intelligence, grace and loyalty. She knew she was being trained to be the next Matriarch.

Meanwhile, as was the tradition, she was married to a minor government official. She and her husband got along reasonably well, and they had three children and raised them in the city. She went to the Women's Palace to have her babies, and she was relieved when all three were deemed healthy enough to live. The girls went to the Women's Palace when they were of the right age to be schooled in women's domestic arts, and the boy went to the government school.

One day, the messenger from the Women's Palace arrived with the message she had been dreading. The Matriarch had called the young woman to take the Matriarch's place. There was no question of her husband releasing her, as this was a tremendous honor. There was only one Matriarch, and his wife had been Chosen.

She was initiated as the Matriarch. She hated it. She did not want to condemn babies because they were not perfect. Though she understood all the arguments, for the first months she wept for days every time she gave the guard a baby to destroy.

She decided she could not continue to kill these imperfect children, so she ordered the guards to give the children away to the poor, to sell them as slaves or dispose of them in other ways—but not to murder them. The babies that were not terminally ill or deformed would live, just not as full clan members. This would allow the clan to stay strong, yet save the children.

Thus, she lived out her life deciding the fate of the children brought to her from the birthing beds. She still did not relish her position but she was resigned to it.

When asked at her death what she thought of her life, she replied, "It was a terrible life to be forced to be the Matriarch and to live with those choices."

When she was given the chance to live her life again and choose differently, the ancestor was ecstatic.

She returned to a point in her life where she met and fell in love with a trader before she was sent to the Women's Palace. Her parents objected to her decision to marry the trader because he was not of their class and did not have sufficient money or status.

She decided to run away with her love, so they married and joined a caravan that traveled across the land bridge to North America. It was a hard life. Her husband hunted and traded. They moved farther south until the weather was warmer and the game was better. During her life she lost several children in childbirth or to accidents. Only one daughter survived to marry and have her own family.

Although she did not have as easy a life as she did in China, she was happy, loved and fulfilled. She chose her husband, her family and her life. On her deathbed, she was happy and fulfilled in this lifetime.

Although the child was not present at the session, the ancestor came forward clearly and was quite eager to choose the new life. Both the mother and I were encouraged by the result. I asked the mother to let me know how the daughter was doing in a few weeks after the new energy was set.

About a month later I talked to the mother. She was so excited to tell me how her daughter had changed. "It's a miracle. She is so much better and happier. She doesn't feel like 'a piece of shit' anymore." The daughter was now able to receive love. The mother showed me a picture the little girl had drawn of a beautiful heart with lovely bright colors in the background. There were no shadows or darkness anywhere. Even family friends had noticed the change in the girl. She had definitely had a change of heart.

Ancestral Lineage Clearing can successfully shift the challenges for a child if necessary. The child's ancestors are as enthusiastic about helping the children as they are about aiding adults. Do not hesitate to ask for assistance if there is a child in your care who could benefit from this type of healing.

About Extraterrestrials

Someone once asked if Ancestral Lineage Clearing would work for them if they were from a different planet. Usually I find most people have had multiple lives on earth, even if they associate their last lifetime with another planet. If they are having earthly difficulties, then it normally comes from an ancestor who lived here and embedded the challenge in a family pattern that the particular individual needs to clear.

Having said that, I had a client, Emma, who was having difficulty resolving her grief after her mother died. She was a lovely woman who had cared for her mother for many years during her last illness, and they had a close relationship. As I took her back into the past she found her ancestors:

Grief

As Emma stepped from the Time Stream onto the bank she moved into a foggy, non-descript landscape. Nothing was clear—no natural forms, buildings, landscapes or shapes appeared. She walked ahead. She felt as if she were going uphill until she reached the flat top.

At the top there were 14 entities. Although somewhat individualized they also seemed to be a group consciousness. Love emanated from them as they welcomed her without words. Emma basked in this feeling for a few moments.

I then encouraged her to ask for what she needed from them. What could they tell her to help her to resolve her grief?

An unspoken message came into her heart and mind from the group. "Forgive your parents and yourself for all."

She understood the message immediately. In the fullness of the moment she knew she needed to go home and process forgiveness for all the hurt, anger, fear, guilt and judgment she still held against her parents and herself from over the years. Then she would be free of the grief.

She thanked the entities and came back to this time and place. A great healing took place.

Clearly these entities were not physical earth beings, or if they were, they were from a time or dimension before, or after, we were in physical form.

Neither of us had anticipated contacting extraterrestrials or beings from another dimension. They appeared when they were needed by Emma, with whom they had a deep and loving connection.

This was an unusual lineage clearing. There was no life story, no altering of probabilities, no choice point and no changing of energies in the past. **There was a huge shift in energy**. Emma learned what she needed and we released her present, intense grieving. After her first stage of grief was lifted, she was able to bask in the love of her parents and enter into the energy of forgiveness the entities has given her.

Foreign Cultures

The first time I received a request from a person of non-Western culture, I was slightly nervous about how well Ancestral Lineage Clearing would work. All my experience had been with Westerners and mixed Native Americans with a background similar to mine. My ego was getting in the way of my confidence in the healing process.

Tiassale was African; he had seen my website and was interested in a session. He had a background in meditation and spiritual healing, and sought to resolve some deep family issues surrounding his ability to move forward in life. His life in Africa was vastly different than mine in America. I meditated and asked Spirit for guidance and support for the Ancestral Lineage Clearing session.

The session resulted in deep healing for Tiassale. He met an ancestor Spirit Guide who went on the journey with him and promised to be with him in the future. He met the ancestor he searched for and the ancestor made a marvelous new choice that resulted in a happy and healthy life. We released the old negative family patterns and reset the new positive energies he found with his ancestors.

No matter your location, background or circumstance, Ancestral Lineage Clearing works. It is an energetic healing practice that will connect you to ancestors. We all have ancestors, they all love us, and we can trust Spirit to guide us to them.

Conclusion

We are intended to overcome family pattern challenges in our lifetimes, either on our own or with assistance. Ancestral Lineage Clearing can assist us in resolving those family issues **that we are meant to clear** so we can live a happy and fulfilling life. Health, happiness, prosperity and love are our birthright on the Earth.

Chapter VII
Destiny

For many, the word *destiny* conveys a curious, even mystical concept. The dictionary defines destiny as "the predetermined, usually inevitable or irresistible course of events." It is a definition that appears to have many interpretations.

For some, **destiny means life is controlled, or even predestined, by external forces over which individuals have little or no say**. There are religions that believe in predestination—the concept that our whole lives are predetermined by God—and that we are here merely to experience and fulfill God's plan with little or no choice in the matter. Most other religions, particularly in the United States, propound the *free will* concept, which says that each person has a choice over each and every action in life and can choose his or her destiny daily.

Depending on your perspective, both are correct. From a metaphysical point of view, we choose our parents and the family we are born into for this lifetime. Therefore, having chosen this body and these parents and ancestors, our destiny has been predetermined **to a certain extent** by preselecting the body, DNA, environment and family in which to grow. This initial choice is with us throughout our life.

Some also believe we enter into a contract before we are born that binds us to what we agreed to do in this lifetime. Buddha agreed to bring a new philosophy to India during his life. Mary agreed to be the mother of Jesus. Lincoln agreed to be President during the Civil War and to be assassinated.

There is some debate as to whether or not we can alter our pre-life contract during our lifetime. Since our higher spiritual self has a much broader perspective of this life than our earthly self does at any exact point in time, it may be hazardous to make alterations without fully considering the implications for our future, and the future of forthcoming generations. I personally know several people who have consciously and successfully chosen to change their life contracts; however, it is a process that requires concentrated spiritual work and dedication.

Once an action has been taken, destiny is set; the irreversible course of events has taken place. If you decided to climb a tree at ten years old and fell and broke your leg, it was your destiny to have a broken leg at that time. **The past is final** (at least as of this timeline). This much is obvious.

Changing the Past in the Present

However, much of what we thought as irreversible from the past can be changed. We can change:

1. Our emotional reaction to the past: pain, fear, anger, resentment, bitterness, hatred;
2. Our attitude or reaction to events of the past: sense of failure, self-esteem, attitudes of revenge;
3. Clinging to the old patterns, beliefs and ways of life that no longer serve us: drinking excessively, overeating, violent behavior, self-destructive behaviors;

4.　　Our physical health patterns: negative eating and exercise patterns, failing to deal with minor health issues that lead to major physical breakdowns, shifting trauma patterns locked in physical structures.

1. Emotional Reactions to the Past

Almost everyone grew up in an environment that caused challenges later in life. If you were an only child, you wanted siblings. If you grew up in a big family, you wanted to be an only child. Every child has issues with his or her parents at one point or another. These childhood memories, challenges, issues, difficulties, problems (or whatever you want to call them) become a part of our stories. We all know people who whine every day about how terrible their life is because of their awful childhood.

It is called growing up. **The past does not control your future**. We all have control over our emotions now, today. I just love the book *It Is Never Too Late to Have a Happy Childhood*, by Claudia Black. This book gives healing messages to adult children who had painful early years.

Teri Mahaney, PhD, does brain repatterning through CD programs called "Change Your Mind," which releases past negative programming and resets thoughts (http://www.changeyourmind.com). She had a *terrible* childhood and made an effort to release all the negative emotions of her past and reset her brain. After she made this change, she went to an intuitive reader, who remarked what a wonderful childhood she had. Teri just laughed and informed the reader that she'd had a dreadful childhood. Dr.

Mahaney had cleared the past energy so that it no longer held her hostage. Now she produces programs to help others to alter their thinking patterns around negative thoughts and behaviors.

If you still cannot see the value of the traumas of your past and the gifts it taught you, then it is time for deep emotional healing. When we do Ancestral Lineage Clearing, we find the basis for the family patterns that continue to exist in generations sometimes for hundreds of years. These patterns are usually based in emotional trauma. **Clearing emotional trauma in the present, frees our future from the immediate past in this lifetime, and makes the clearing of any other issue from prior generations so much easier.**

When we can look back at our past with objectivity and embrace the gifts of the adversity we have overcome, we become proud of our achievements instead of resentful of our victimhood. As we no longer identify with being a victim, our energy is freed to maintain our creative life power.

2. Attitudes about Our Past

The most effective way I have seen people affect their present is to change their attitude about the past. Many people lost their jobs in the recession of 2008 and its aftermath. At the time of this writing the unemployment rate is still about 10%. A common reaction to prolonged unemployment is depression, a sense of failure, hopelessness and a loss of self-esteem.

I know; I've been there. I was unemployed for almost a year. My savings were gone. I was borrowing money from friends for the rent. The situation was pretty grim. I was not depressed, however; I trusted in the Divine and just continued to make calls and pursue my career, intuitively *KNOWING* I would succeed. My attitude remained positive (mostly) with the help of my friends, books and resources at my disposal, and the positive commitments I continued to use (circulating money, meditating, asking for support from my friends, going to positive gatherings).

Some of the helpful stories I encountered are now commonly known, such as the fact that Elvis was a failed truck driver who had to play music to earn a living. Busby Berkley, the great New York Broadway Producer of the 1930s and 40s, went bankrupt three times putting on extravagant productions, but continued to return to producing and finding investors to back him. When Edison was asked how he felt about failing 1,000 times to find the right filament for the light bulb, he replied, "I succeeded 1,000 times in finding filaments that didn't work in a light bulb."

So, how our past affects our future depends upon our attitude. **Tomorrow does not depend on what happened yesterday.** We can take the information we learned yesterday and tweak it today for the better. More entrepreneurs arise from unemployment to create new products and new lives than from staid corporate jobs. If we clear the past of its negative connotations, we are free to learn from it instead of remaining burdened by it.

3. Clinging to Old Patterns, Beliefs and Ways of Life

Change is difficult for all of us. The present is predictable, comfortable and familiar. Change is unpredictable, uncomfortable and unfamiliar. It can also be exciting, interesting and thrilling.

We all know people stuck in the past. They do not want to see innovation even if it will improve circumstances for themselves or others. Are you living in your parents' home, figuratively speaking? Do you find yourself using their expressions, going the same places they went, saying the same things to your children, believing the same things they did? Have you consciously made that choice or have you just fallen into your family's old pattern and not considered how it has affected you?

If we live the way our ancestors lived we are clinging to their patterns. Some of their patterns are positive and helpful. My family patterns of honesty, cleanliness, hard work, family love, spiritual devotion and responsible money handling are all good traits. Other family patterns needed to be cleared because of their adverse effect on me, as well as other family members. I do not hold onto the family patterns of prejudice, racism, intolerance, abuse, secrets, ill health, violence and poverty. These ancestral wounds needed to be cleared in order for me to find peace and love in my own life.

Catherine came to me because she was having difficulty dealing with her older parents and in other parts of her life with people who insisted she do things the "right way," or the way they had always been done. Basically, they wanted her to conform to their notions of her role. She wanted to clear this pattern from her life.

Conformity

As she stepped from the Time Stream she walked into a Native American village and spotted a young man. He was clearly a warrior, yet he was taking care of his father and his other younger siblings. He was the responsible adult in the family. His father was admonishing him about cleaning up and taking care of the children. Meanwhile, the father sat and smoked his pipe and gossiped with the old men.

The young man clearly resented his father in this arrangement. He had taken on this responsibility after his mother died, as was the way of the village. In his tribe the young took care of the older generation. When parents died, the eldest child took over the responsibility for the family.

Though he had numerous brothers and sisters, the young man's father gave him no assistance at all. He was expected to do everything—the hunting, cooking, cleaning, child-care—and wait on his father hand and foot.

The older children helped by fishing and gathering food. They also helped with the younger ones, but he still had to watch and make sure they didn't wander off. This went on for years. He felt he had the weight of the world on his shoulders.

Eventually he married his sweetheart after most of the children left home. Then they began having their own children. It wasn't that he did not love his children; he just felt that his burdens and responsibilities were as great as ever. His wife certainly helped, but he still had to care for his father, and now his wife and their children. He and his father were constantly at odds, and they grew bitter and resentful towards one another.

He did what was expected of him, and was known as a good son, husband and father. The elders praised him for being a good man. They didn't know how much bitterness, resentment and anger he carried in his heart against everyone for the burdens he carried.

When he died he was relieved. He didn't have to work anymore. He didn't have to take care of anyone any more. He could lay his burdens down at last.

The client saw the result of conforming to everyone's expectations. Everyone else was happy, but her ancestor had led a miserable and unhappy life. We then asked the ancestor to go to the Choice Point in his life and choose differently. This was the result:

The young warrior was helping his father with the younger children as he always did. His father told him that it was his responsibility now to take over the family.

His mother was dead and it was time the father moved on to the men's elder circle.

The young man protested. "I'm too young to take on this family. What about my own family? I'm not supposed to take over until I'm older and I have established my own life. I just became a hunter. I'm not ready."

The father wouldn't hear of waiting until his son grew up. He did not want the responsibility of raising all the children now that his wife was gone. It was tradition that the eldest child must take over. His son was old enough. It was his obligation. As the father, he had the right to retire from family management.

The son knew there was no appeal; it just worked that way. All his relatives from his granny and his aunties and uncles to the Elder Council would sympathize, but it was customary for the eldest to accept this family duty. There was no way out except to run away.

It was unheard of to leave the village because it was dangerous to be on one's own. He knew he would have to travel far from the neighboring tribes of the same culture. So he planned his escape, taking his weapons and as much food as he could carry. After many moons of traveling, he found a tribe that knew nothing of his village, and they welcomed a new, young warrior.

He stayed and eventually fell in love and married a beautiful young maiden. They had several children and were respected members of their community.

After many years, when their youngest was old enough to travel long distances, the man decided to return home. They said good-bye to his wife's family and the village and left.

When he and his family arrived home they were welcomed with open arms. Everyone was so happy to see him. They had been convinced he had died a long time ago.

His father was also pleased to see him. All the former bickering and resentment was gone. His father had taken a new wife, raised the rest of the children, and had been busy and happy in the interim.

The young man and his family stayed with his tribe until he died. He was happy with his family. When the time came for him to take care of his father at the end of his life, he was content to do so. He was capable of the responsibility at that time of his life. He and his father had developed a love and respect for each other that they never had in the prior lifetime.

Catherine sensed that the responsibilities she was being asked to assume or that were being imposed upon her were not right at the time. Other peoples' *shoulds* were not her obligations. This Ancestral Lineage Clearing released the wounds of her ancestor who had been bound by the ties of his family and culture. Catherine gave her ancestor the opportunity to free them both as well as all future generations from a binding conformity improperly imposed on them by others.

I am disturbed when I see people falling into the same unhappy pattern of their parents or the older generations. When a client asks for help to change an unhappy family behavior pattern, I am excited to be able to help the client and his or her family. Letting go of the ancestral past will tremendously unburden our lives.

4. Physical health patterns

Health is not predetermined at birth. Our genetic make-up gives us a **predisposition** to certain dis-eases based on our ancestors' health profile, but their health profile is not ours. Even if we had identical genes, we would not have the same illnesses. The impact of the dis-eases would be different because of our environment, the food we eat, the messages our brain receives and our education.

If our parents had heart disease, the treatment they received was much different than the treatment of heart dis-ease today. Medical science is continually advancing. Moreover, subsequent generations have significantly more information about heart dis-ease than earlier ones. We can be proactive about diet, exercise, mental imagery, meditation, prayer, herbs, supplements and medication.

Health is also subject to family patterns. **Illness is an attitude and a lifestyle**. Stress, bad eating habits, the lack of exercise, poor body image, lack of discipline and ignoring self-care, are all directly related to environment and family values. Clearing these ancestral patterns and altering the messages of your spiritual, mental, emotional and physical bodies will have an enormous impact on your health.

Our parents both had a history of heart disease. My sister, Julie, had her first heart attack at the age of 43. She had been working spiritually on her heart chakra (a spiritual energy center based in the heart) for several years, knowing her heart was blocked. In her younger years she smoked heavily, drank alcohol excessively, never exercised, and her diet was terrible. Although she had worked diligently for several years, her heart had sustained so much damage there was too much to unclog energetically by the time she knew enough to clear it.

She had another heart attack a year later because the doctors could not stabilize her heart; she was allergic the usual medication they normally used for things like blood thinners, beta blockers and cholesterol-lowering drugs. While she was monitoring herself energetically and the doctors were working to stabilize her, she went into congestive heart failure. It was during this time I was learning about and evolving Ancestral Lineage Clearing.

I did an Ancestral Lineage Clearing on the maternal side of the family. My mother had her first angina attack at 27, a major heart attack with damage to her heart at about age 33 (see Chapter I). After completing the Ancestral Lineage Clearing, Julie came out of her congestive heart failure within two weeks. It has now been three years and her heart is stable. She is still healing, and her heart grows stronger every day.

Difference between Past Life and Ancestral Lineage Clearing

Some people have asked about the difference between past life regression and Ancestral Lineage Clearing. **Often, when clients search for the ancestor who initiated a pattern of dysfunction, they find they were the ancestor in a past life. However, this is not necessarily the case in every Ancestral Lineage Clearing.**

In past life regression, a client is searching for one or more past lives that are affecting his or her present life. For example, if a person is afraid of the water, maybe he drowned in a past life as a sailor or had a life in which he was killed in a flood. If this issue affects only the client and no one else in the family, it is suitable for altering in past life regression therapy.

In Ancestral Lineage Clearing, the client and practitioner look together at issues that affect not only the client but other members of the family. If the person has an abandonment issue and observes that his mother, aunts, grandmother and siblings have also played out this issue in their lives, then it is not merely a singular issue in *his* life, but a familial issue that has a heritage basis.

The primary difference between past life regression and Ancestral Lineage Clearing is that past life regression only affects an individual's wounds and challenges, whereas Ancestral Lineage Clearing the issues affecting the individual also appear in other family members.

We are all individuals and we must consider each person's situation separately.

Furthermore, if the client has done past life regression, soul retrieval, healing work, and spiritual counseling, and has worked through the same or other emotional issues without resolution, then the challenge may be a familial issue that needs to be addressed because it rests in the DNA coding of the body.

If an issue arises in one lifetime and is concluded satisfactorily, then there is no carryover into the next lifetime or generation. Even if the issue continues into the next lifetime or generation and is completed, it may not even then become encoded in the genetic pattern.

If the challenge remains constant and ongoing during a soul's continuation through many lifetimes, at some point the propensity toward the same challenge is set in the DNA. Until and unless someone in the genetic line breaks the genetic code by solving the problem and unlocking the code, it continues to pass down to the following generations.

Let's discuss this in simple genetic terms. If we are growing peas and this year there is excessive rain, the peas may grow a tougher pod to protect the peas inside from getting too much moisture; i.e., cause and effect. The next year the peas have a tougher pod even though it is dryer, because the seeds do not know what to expect. If the next year is still dry, the peas will then have a regular pod. The tougher pod did not get set into the DNA of the pea strain, because it was not needed since the challenge of too much rain was resolved. If rain continued to fall excessively for a number of years, the gene for the thicker pod would have been established in the DNA of the peas, because it would have been a necessary protective device.

Resistance
Client Resistance

Although clients have decided Ancestral Lineage Clearing will benefit them that decision alone does not mean they are completely ready to face deep-seated issues that have controlled their lives. Even though they know they must change, they must be **ready and willing** to change the old ways on a conscious and subconscious level. Change is uncomfortable and unknown, and unexpected things will occur. Therefore, resistance is bound to arise.

Resistance is merely a fear response. It does not mean a person does not desire to move forward. It is the body, mind or emotional defense mechanism to protect the status quo. If the issue at hand has been set in the family's genetic pattern for generations, it will try to defend its place in the system.

In his book *Callings*, Gregg LeVoy says:

The desire to protect ourselves from change probably does more harm to the flowing of human life and spirit than almost any other choice, but it is imperative to understand something about security: It isn't secure! Everything about security is contrary to the central fact of existence: Life changes. By trying to shelter ourselves from change, we isolate ourselves from living. By avoiding risk we may feel safe and secure—or at least experience a tolerable parody thereof—but we don't avoid the harangues of our consciences.

The genetic pattern was initially set for a reason, usually as a defense mechanism arising from fear, danger or self-protection. Until the clearing ceremony is complete and your spirit reassures your body, mind and emotions that you are safe, resistance will try to protect you.

Bob came to me with relationship issues. When he was born he had been given up for adoption by his teenage mother, and was adopted by her parents, who were in their 50s. His adopted mother (grandmother) had a heart attack when he was six, and he was placed in foster care. His foster father later developed health problems, as well as becoming an alcoholic. Bob spent the next twelve years in foster care, only visiting his grandparents (adopted family) occasionally because he was deemed "too difficult to handle."

When he was in his 30s Bob found his birth mother and learned that he had step-siblings. His father had abandoned his biological mother, and she, too, had ongoing abandonment issues. The client and his birth mother never developed a relationship. He was in his 40s by the time he came to see me, had never been married, had had difficulties with all his relationships, and was ready to change.

As we went into the session he had no problem identifying his abandonment issue. His mother had abandoned him, his adopted grandparents had abandoned him, and his many foster homes had abandoned him. This was clearly a generational issue more prevalent on his mother side.

Abandonment

Bob walked onto the sand at sundown and saw the golden glow of the desert shining on the great pyramid. Standing in its shadow was a beautiful woman in pure white linen waiting for him. Ankor, dressed in full Egyptian military gear with armor, helmet and a sword, as was his accustomed daily habit, came out of the palms toward her. Ankor approached the woman. Bob could feel the love and conflict in Ankor's heart.

"I have come to tell you good-bye."

"Why? Where are you going?" She asked.

"I have been assigned to the southern frontier to command the new fortress. I will be gone for a long time, and I am setting you free," he replied.

"I can come with you."

"No. I cannot have you there distracting me from my duties. The frontier is dangerous and no place for women. As commander of our forces I have to build the Egyptian fortress from the ground and subdue the outlying area. Your place is here and I cannot take you away from it."

She flung herself into his arms and sobbed, "I love you. I don't want to part. I will wait."

"Don't be silly," he said harshly. "I could be gone for one year or twenty. You could

be an old woman by the time I get back. It is better to break it off now."

He kissed her brow, pushed her away and stalked back to the barracks, abandoning her to the sand and darkness of the night.

The next morning he led his troops south to the border of the Upper Kingdom. The border was in chaos. Ankor and his forces were kept busy with the regular skirmishes in the border towns and regions. Occasionally, there were major battles with the neighboring tribes and villages seeking the riches of the cities and the caravans that traded all types of goods with them—food, clothing, fabrics, jewelry, rugs, metals and weapons.

Over the next seven years he built a mighty fortress and a mightier army of the Pharaoh's professional troops and the local recruits. He trained them to guard, fight and find the enemy until the cities and borders were secure. Pharaoh finally recalled him to the palace and named him General in a ceremony befitting his accomplishments. His father would have been proud. He merely felt numb.

Ankor continued his career as a general in the Pharaoh's army during peacetime. He married and had two children, accumulated wealth, and died with his wife and children surrounding him. He was content, but still felt unfulfilled, dissatisfied and unloved.

At this point, I requested that Bob ask his ancestor to return to the point in time where he had a choice—where he could have made a difference in his life. Bob did so, and his ancestor moved back to the time when he confronted the woman at the pyramid.

[This didn't quite feel right to me.]

I ask, "So, what choice does he make or have to make now?"

Bob says, "He has to choose whether to leave her."

"So what does he do?"

Bob replies, "He takes her in his arms and kisses her and tells her it will be alright, and he stays."

I then ask Bob, "Is this what you would do, or is this what Ankor would do?"

Bob says, "This is what I would do."

It was clear that Bob was not ready to complete his abandonment issue yet, and we broke the session at this time. I did sound and energy releasing on his chakras and cleared some energy blocks that were preventing him from reaching his ancestor.

Again, we went back to Egypt and I asked Bob to find Ankor. We went into Ankor's life. Bob asked Ankor to go back to the life-changing *Choice Point* in his life.

This time, Ankor went back to his childhood when his father was making arrangements to apprentice him in the army with a relative.

Ankor felt his stomach clench. His mother was crying, because she knew how sensitive her son was and that this was not the right place for him. Ankor stepped up to his father and said,

"Father, I cannot be a soldier. That is not my place."

No one had ever defied Ankor's father, and particularly not in front of others. "Well, young man, if you don't go into the army, just what do you think you're going to do?"

"I want to be a scribe to the Pharaoh."

Ankor's cousin spoke up and said, "Well, now, almost anyone can be a soldier but it takes a mighty special person to be a scribe. Do you think you could really do it, young man?"

Ankor spoke right up, "Of course I can."

Thereafter, Ankor had a totally different life. His parents hadn't abandoned him to the army life. He continued to live at home, even though his father resented the fact that he did not go into the army. He felt supported and loved by his mother during the rest of his childhood.

He did well as a scribe and eventually did become scribe to the Pharaoh. He met the woman at the pyramid and married her. They lived very happily and had two children. He became a wealthy man, and died happy and fulfilled.

He did not abandon his love as a result of the army's commands. He made a different choice and chose a different probability without abandonment by his family, and without his having to abandon his true love. Now the issue of abandonment is no longer in the energetic pattern of Ankor's descendants. Bob now feels free from his own abandonment issues.

Ancestor Resistance

Although I have never had an ancestor refuse to make a better choice when offered the opportunity, I have encountered confusion and uncertainty with several ancestors when presented with the offer to change their life.

Control Issue

In one particular session, Kelsey was dealing with an issue of family control. As we went back in time she found her controlling ancestor in Britain, around the Hadrian's Wall area at the time the Romans were conquering the Picts.

In her ancestor's original lifetime, her tribe had been virtually wiped out in a horrendous battle that had left her ancestor and her children virtual slaves to the Roman occupiers. She never allowed herself to grieve for her husband, or for family or friends who had died in battle or who were later killed by the Roman soldiers.

The ancestor felt she had to control every thought, action and behavior of her children in order for her heritage to survive. This manipulation and control was maintained throughout the ensuing generations straight down to Kelsey's time, causing family estrangement and resentment.

When we reached the conversation about asking her ancestor to go back to the *Choice Point* and choose another probability for her life, **her ancestor could not conceive of how her life might have been different**. Initially, she considered dying in the battle with the Romans (the women in the tribe fought alongside the men). But dying would not have resulted in a more meaningful life, and so I encouraged the ancestor to search further for a different point.

She thought about running away from the tribe with her children, but her heart's desire was in preserving her heritage, and this was not an acceptable choice.

Kelsey: Are you willing to go back and change this life and make a different life for you and your children?

Ancestor: Yes; I could kill myself, or fight until I died and all my children and all my people died.

Ariann: Tell her she doesn't have to die. She can go back and make another choice for her life and her children.

Kelsey relays the information and tells her to go back to the Choice Point.

Ancestor: I don't know what that is. I have to fight. I won't let those Romans take my children.

Ariann: Tell her she can go back before the battle or even earlier, and choose to leave the village and not fight; she can move away earlier; she can move after the battle, or even go back in her childhood and make a different choice. Tell her to relax and breathe. Let her heart show the way.

Kelsey again relays this information.

Ancestor: Oh. (Pause.) After the battle I gather up all the children and all who are left in the village. We agree to move south to another village of Britons. They are not of the same people, but they are more like our people than these foreign Romans. We must preserve our way of life.

Kelsey: Why is this so important?

Ancestor: The Romans do not value the Earth Spirits. They bring their foreign gods and steal everything from us. We must teach our children the old ways to keep them strong and keep the land strong for the People.

Other tribal members, who were injured, elderly or sick, died along the way. She was heartsick at the loss but forged ahead.

In this second lifetime she allowed herself to grieve. Her anger at the Romans did not fester and eat at her soul. Eventually they found another British tribe with a similar heritage. Their tribes merged and she became a teacher of old traditions and the legacies of their people.

It was a hard life, and there was always danger from Romans and other conquering neighbors. She kept their heritage alive with the younger generations and had no need to control her children or anyone else. She fulfilled her desire to keep the tribe alive and separate from Roman influence.

The ancestor was much more satisfied in this lifetime. Since this was a time of religious and cultural disruption for her people, there was no way to escape the chaos of the surrounding world. However, her new choice was the most satisfactory option to fulfill her life purpose and allow her to love her children.

Kelsey incorporated this new energy in her present life and no longer felt controlled by her mother and other relatives. She could now be free since she no longer felt bound by the fear from the past. Kelsey could make her choices with a clear and happy heart.

Conclusion

Destiny does not mean our life is a foregone conclusion. We can alter our pre-birth contract with our Higher Self. Even if we do not choose to do this, we can still change our attitudes, behaviors, belief systems and perceptions about the past. By changing our perceptions we can change our emotional state of happiness, love, joy—and even health.

Chapter VIII
Choosing Ancestral Lineage Clearing

The Healing Process

When we are first introduced to the healing process in life, we generally start with the physical body since it gets our attention first. As a child, we may fall down and skin our knee. It bleeds and hurts; we scream and cry. Mother comes and tends to it, and our knee gets better.

As we grow older our pain becomes more sophisticated. Pain gets our attention by manifesting in our bodies as injury or illness. If we are stressed, we get headaches, upset stomachs, stiff necks, sore backs and a variety of aches and pains.

If stress goes untreated the physical symptoms become worse, perhaps manifesting as migraines, ulcers, TMJ (temporomandibular disorders, or tight jaws,) pulled tendons, herniated disks, or sleepless nights, which can cause disorientation, car accidents, and a variety of other stress-related illnesses and injuries.

Many of the terminal dis-eases of modern life, such as heart dis-ease, diabetes, cancer, mental illnesses, car accidents, etc., are the result of our high-paced, high-pressure life styles. Disease is literally a dis-ease of our body—a body not at ease with itself.

Pain is merely a signal from our body telling us to *Pay Attention*, as something is not working correctly. We need to stop and listen to our body tell us what is not at ease in our body and in our life.

When is Ancestral Lineage Clearing Not Appropriate?
Acute, Initial, Emotional Attacks

A lot of pain is not necessarily physical. Ask anyone who has just broken up with a lover. The pain is real and tangible; we feel it in our body, mind, emotions and soul. The sobs are not only from the emotional body, but from our mind spinning over the past and an imagined or hoped for future. Physical pain results from the emotional stress, such as the stomach churning, the head hurting, and the gut-wrenching, soul-tearing physical pain of being torn from the one you love.

If we are having trouble at work with the boss, it affects more than just the mind. Our muscles tighten whenever the boss walks by or asks for a meeting. Our stomachs may drop whenever we see a memo cross the desk with our name on it. If we cannot resolve the conflict within a certain amount of time, we may lose sleep at night and not want to come to work in the morning.

These are the **initial, acute stages in the dis-ease process**. In the above instances, we are usually able to identify the cause of the physical distress as something that is not physical in origin. We can then deal with the physical symptoms so that they don't become worse, while simultaneously coping with the mental and emotional distress of the current situation.

Some things, like the broken heart, can initially be mended by time, particularly with the love and support of friends and family. The difficulties with the work situation could have multiple remedies depending upon the conflict, and many different resources may be utilized in seeking a resolution.

Counseling, mental health therapy and spiritual guidance are excellent resources to learn coping skills in crises and acute stages of distress. Counselors of all types can help us recognize how to observe our lives, in order to understand what part we play in creating situations in our lives that cause grief, anger, conflict and rejection. "We create our reality" is an old adage that is truer than we may think.

In the above, Ancestral Lineage Clearing is not a first healing option of choice. These examples are clearly matters that need to be addressed promptly, practically and situationally.

However, if your heart is constantly getting broken, and this is the fifth job you've had where you are in conflict with your boss, then Resetting of Family Patterns using Ancestral Lineage Clearing may be appropriate for you.

Exercise: Identify an acute physical or emotional situation in your life that you resolved for which Ancestral Lineage Clearing was NOT appropriate.

Severe Injury, Illness in Acute Stage

We do not always see the causal relationship behind dis-eases like cancer, diabetes, chronic fatigue, fibromyalgia, heart dis-ease or many other long-term disabling illnesses. **Even injuries like home and car accidents, falls, and workplace**

injuries are often the result of factors other than the ones we initially observe.

A psychiatrist once commented to me that he was not surprised when one of his patients was in a car accident. The patient had been telling him for months that 'He felt like an accident waiting to happen.' Well, the patient didn't have to wait for the accident to happen anymore.

Cancer, heart dis-ease, diabetes or chronic illness should be treated immediately by a health care practitioner. Many health conditions are life-threatening and there are many types of physical and mental healing available to care for these conditions. **Treatment on the physical level (and perhaps the spiritual, emotional and mental plane) is critical in acute stages** and to deal with depression, confusion and the stress that accompanies major illnesses. Follow-up care is necessary to keep the physical condition stabilized while energetic advanced work can take place. Comfort care is necessary to relieve pain and restore energy after severe illnesses have debilitated the body.

Ancestral Lineage Clearing is again not the first option. Clients should be in a stable medical condition before pursuing Ancestral Lineage Clearing. Clients need sufficient strength and energy to devote attention to inner care. If our physical and emotional conditions distract from taking care of our inner selves, we are not yet ready to face the heritage issues that may be brewing in our lives.

When is Ancestral Lineage Clearing Most Effective?

There are at least four conditions I have identified for Ancestral Lineage Clearing to be the most effective:

1. When we have a **dysfunctional pattern** in our life, or in the lives of our family members, that is holding us back from being happy or having the best life can offer;

2. When we have a **chronic condition** that seems resistant to treatment and has an emotional, mental or spiritual component that appears related in some ways to our background, environment or family;

3. When there are **family dis-ease or addiction patterns** that we want to avoid or to change in order to improve our life in the present;

4. When we have reached a **plateau** in our life and **want to move upward in order to achieve our goals**, despite doing our personal growth work and emotional healing. We may feel restless and anxious knowing that our life could be better, freer and more joyous; but we feel the block or hindrance lying somewhere in the family's past.

These types of issues are most amenable to change in Ancestral Lineage Clearing.

1. Dysfunctional Patterns

What are dysfunctional patterns? Dysfunctional is defined as "failing to perform the function that is normally expected in a social context, or relating badly." A pattern means you do the same thing repeatedly.

For example, we see a pattern if a person cannot seem to keep a job, or in someone who often fails in maintaining relationships. Or, if we cannot seem to make enough money to support ourselves or family, no matter how hard we try.

If we keep making the same mistake time after time, even when we have sought help and have attempted other solutions, we may be ready for an Ancestral Lineage Clearing.

Let me be clear, **this is not a remedy for failure.** If you have just been divorced, lost your business, and your family is not talking to you, Ancestral Lineage Clearing will not solve your problems.

Identifying and changing patterns is what we are searching for in our lives. If you've been in counseling and identified your co-dependency traits and then corrected this pattern, but you still cannot seem to hang onto relationships even with friends, then this may be an issue from your family's heritage that goes deeper than co-dependency. This is particularly true if your parents did not have a good marriage or a lot of friends, had co-dependency issues, etc. Look around at your life, as well as the lives of your parents, siblings and relatives, and see if a similar issue arose in their lives, too. This is an ideal issue for Ancestral Lineage Clearing.

Steve came to reset a family pattern about being misunderstood and rejected for who he was.

Misunderstood

As Steve went ashore from the Time Stream he found himself in a forest and heard someone chopping wood. He saw a large man chopping firewood, and followed him back to a cottage in the forest where the man lived with his wife and children. The man wore hand-woven clothes and leather boots, and the cottage looked as if he had built it himself. Clearly, the family had recently moved into the forest, which was within walking distance of a village, but outside the formal boundary.

The man's name was Hugo. Hugo had been a farmer, loving the land and outdoor life. He had his own farm, but after several years of bad weather, spoiled crops and dismal markets, he had failed to succeed. He had given up and moved the family to the forest to see if he could raise his family alone without having to make payments to the landowner.

They had a hard life. Hugo hunted and fished for food while his wife and children gathered fruit, greens and herbs from the forest. He tried to clear a small patch of land for a garden or for farming, but it was hard work clearing the huge old forest trees and the dense underbrush. They sold skins and herbs and whatever else they could spare in the village for necessities. During the winters, starvation was always close at hand. After several years and two children later, he gave up and went back to their original village, with his tail between his legs.

*There was no work to be had as a farmer;
all the local farmers had all the laborers
they needed. Hugo was forced to work for
the shoemaker, and he and his family lived
above the shop. Hugo made shoes indoors
all day and his wife dealt with the customers
if the owner wasn't around.*

*Hugo was known as grumpy and
unapproachable in the community. He did
not get along very well with his children
because he was gone all day, and angry and
frustrated after working indoors during the
daylight hours. Although he loved his wife,
he was so unhappy with his life that he
pushed her away and closed down his
emotions. At his death, he felt as though he
had been a failure, and that he had lived a
wasted, unhappy life. He was ready to leave
this earthly plain.*

When Steve asked Hugo if he was willing to
live this life over and make different choices, he was
overjoyed to have the opportunity to change this life.

*When Hugo looked for the Choice Point in
his life he discovered it while farming. He
loved his farm but he knew he was not
succeeding. He knew he had to do
something differently. He swallowed his
pride and went to his father and his
brothers and asked for help. They were
happy to lend him a hand. [In the prior life
there had been no contact with his original
family; Steve picked up no information
regarding Hugo's biological family at all.]*

They helped him with the planting and harvesting. They gave him advice about what crops to plant and how to sell them at market. In a few years he was able to buy a wagon and mule and sell his produce and grain in the next town. He was happy and fulfilled, and was known as an honest and hearty fellow.

Sometimes his wife would go with him to market. She would advise him where to sell and how to market their goods. They became prosperous, bought more land and grew even more crops. Their whole family benefited. His sons tended the land when they grew up, as he and his wife did more and more of the marketing to the bigger towns. Hugo died happy and wealthy with his extended family surrounding him.

Steve learned to ask for help and to let his family and friends know of his struggles and desires. It is better to ask for what you need, even if it is difficult, than to struggle alone and shut out those who can, and will, help you attain your life purpose.

Poverty consciousness is an overwhelming, dysfunctional pattern in today's society. We get so many messages about our worth in the world based upon how much money we have. Many people are locked into hopeless, dead-end jobs they hate, because they have no sense of self-worth and cannot see themselves moving into a bright prosperous future.

One day early in the development of the Ancestral Lineage Clearing process when I was feeling particularly hopeless without any visible reason, I sat down to meditate, and I asked to see the reason for this issue in my life. When I was deeply into the meditation I received this vision:

Poverty Consciousness

I was deep in the past. I was cold—the deep, deep cold that penetrates bones down to your soul. I could not remember the last time I was warm. It was dark, and the tiny speck of light coming from somewhere just above my head – no, not above – on my head, showed only more black. There was sound not too far away– a sense of the earth groaning and muffled voices murmuring. I held something hard in my hands, and looked down. My hands were black with dirt. I held a pick—sharp, long and heavy. There was a pile of rocks at my feet and a half-filled cart not far away.

All of a sudden I knew, just intuitively *knew*, where I was and what was happening.

This man was my father's ancestor. He had a wife and children. He once had a farm, but after years of farming it had failed as a result of drought, disease and wars, during which the crops had been burned. He couldn't even raise enough food on the land to feed his family, and when he could not pay his farm share to the lord, he and his family were forced to leave.

This was a long, long time ago, centuries at least.

His only choice was to work in the mines or leave. And how could he leave his beloved Wales, the land of his ancestors and rocks and sea? His heart would break and his children would never know the land of their heritage.

He went to work at the mine. It was worse than the laird. Now the mine owned them, body and soul. The mine owned the hovel they lived in, the food they ate, the clothes they wore. His children worked at the mine hauling water, sorting rock sizes, and running errands. His wife made clothes to sell at the mine store and kept the babe at her side.

Still, they didn't make enough money to pay for what little they ate, or for the terribly high rent. The mine always told him he owed more and more. It was hard for him to tell since he could not read. By taking this job he had sold his soul, and he had sold his family and the next generation, and perhaps the next, to the mine, too. They had slaved for years, only to get deeper into debt.

Why had I searched for this ancestor? My life was good. I always had enough money to meet my bills. I lived in a comfortable and beautiful home. I had a newer car. I had friends and family whom I loved, and I was well loved too. I knew a significant relationship was coming into my life. All was well.

But I always had this **feeling** of hopelessness. Life was oppressive and would beat me down no matter what I did. No matter how much money I had, no matter how much love I had, I felt something was missing. It was never enough. There was always someone or something watching over me who would take it away. I frequently had visions of war, poverty and starvation, even though I had never missed a meal.

This is why I searched. Why I felt disaster was near when there was no rational explanation for this "feeling?" Chronic depression and poverty ran in my family. One of my family members constantly says: "Life is shit and then you die." I've been trying to get him to change his language for years to no avail. He is still stuck in poverty and depression.

After this meditation I clearly saw the reason for my sense of hopelessness. Here was this ancestor from my father's side of the family. He could not make a living at farming so he made a decision to change. He made the best choice available to him, and then his family was even worse off. His whole life and the lives of his wife and children were filled with loss, pain and drudgery. This pain had been transmitted to and through his children to me, his present descendant.

I also knew that this sense of hopelessness was pervasive in my family. Poverty was a continuing challenge with all the members of my generation, as well as with aunts, uncles and cousins. After this meditation I looked at both sides of the family and realized that poverty was an issue on my mother's side of the family as well. So I went into a meditation again and looked for the ancestor on my mother's side who first encountered this situation with hopelessness around money and survival issues.

Slavery and Survival

I saw a woman being beaten by a huge, blond Northman in the cold mud. It was somewhere in middle Europe a long time ago. She was a slave. She whimpered but she knew not to make too much noise or he would beat her more. They liked to have the slaves scream or kick back. He hit her a few more times with his fist, screamed at her in his barbaric tongue and motioned for her to hurry with the water. It was good that she was no longer young or pretty or she would be serving in the big tents as a sex slave as well.

She was just a drudge, but she was worried about her daughter, who would be old enough in a couple of years to be handed over to the warriors when she was 13 or 14—if she lived that long. Now she only fetched and carried. The little ones did the small chores of feeding the chickens and pigs, carrying out slop jars and cleaning out the garbage. She hardly ever saw them.

Only a few short months ago she was a wife and mother, and head of her own household rich with horses, pigs and chickens of her own. She had been respected as a woman of her clan, teaching others the ways of their life as they roamed the land taking only what they needed. Her tribe roamed a wide area with others of their kind as they had for thousands of years. Her family liked roaming the plains and mountains.

That is, until the ravaging North men with their bloody iron swords and pikes came thundering over the mountains, killing the men and enslaving the women and children. They tortured and burned those who tried to escape as a lesson to others. Now, her life and the lives of her children were an endless horror of beatings, starvation and humiliation. There was no escape, no freedom and no joy in this life. She would die if she did not have to protect her children.

I now understood why I felt like my life had always seemed so hopeless, and why I often had feelings of helplessness even though I knew I wasn't helpless. Although my choices had taken me to a place of freedom and happiness, I still carried the energy of ancestral heritage of both my father's and my mother's lineages.

I cleared both of these ancestors' energies and I felt so much better. The restlessness and anxiety were gone. When I learned the advanced technique of resetting new energy, I set new energy in my energy field of prosperity, abundance, helpfulness and resources. Now I always feel there are positive alternatives available at every point in my life.

Family poverty is an ideal area for Ancestral Lineage Clearing.

Exercise: Consider either side of your family, either the maternal or paternal side, determine if there are any negative family patterns, and write down these patterns. Are these/Is this family pattern(s) interfering with your ability to function or find joy and happiness in your life? Have you overcome any dysfunctional family pattern from either side of the family?

2. Chronic Conditions

After an illness, injury or trauma passes beyond the acute stage, at some point health professional use the term *chronic*. This means not only long lasting, but chronic dis-eases or conditions can sometimes cause a long term change in the body chemistry or physical condition.

For example, if we break an ankle and have it in a hard cast for six weeks, we may have resulting hip, back, shoulder and neck problems, because we are twisting when we walk by throwing all our weight onto our other foot. If our ankle is permanently twisted, we may have chronic pain in our hip, back, shoulder and neck if we do not later learn how to move correctly, because favoring our ankle has thrown our entire body out of alignment.

Moreover, chronic conditions tend to arise when there is an emotional component to the physical injury or dis-ease. A spiritual counselor friend calls chronic fatigue the "I hate my husband but can't admit it" dis-ease. She says that most of her clients with chronic fatigue are women who are in dead-end marriages and can't seem to find the courage to leave. They escape through chronic fatigue. Now, I personally do not believe all chronic fatigue sufferers have this same issue, but many dis-eases do have psychological or emotional components.

Chronic health issues often fall within this category. The initial accident or injury may be simple or straight-forward, but may then be followed by complications, infections, secondary conditions or other components that compound the primary diagnosis or condition. All of a sudden, a simple broken ankle is into a second year of treatment, and what may appear to be interminable treatments, surgeries and physical therapies.

Some issues are emotionally or psychologically based. A lifelong issue of giving away our power to authority figures, or not standing up for ourselves, may be a chronic condition. Lack-of-power issues that we have seemly been addressed through counseling—spiritually, mentally or emotionally—may be still present, and can potentially be, cleared through Ancestral Lineage Clearing.

At one time I was training a staff member how to operate some new files and procedures. I told her on at least three occasions to schedule an appointment with me so I could review the files with her. She never set up the appointment, and six months later we lost the client because this staff member never acted on the files. As an adult, this was her responsibility. She could not ask for help, or tell me she couldn't do the work, or even set an appointment to discuss the matter. I wish I had known about Ancestral Lineage Clearing then, as it probably would have helped both of us.

3. Family Dis-ease or Addiction Patterns

My older brother had three stints put into his heart at 53 years old. He discovered his heart condition when he went in for a life insurance physical. The doctor discovered he had had a heart attack about ten years before and now some arteries were blocked.

This was definitely a family issue since both our parents had had heart conditions. This health issue was most strongly on our maternal side, so I did an Ancestral Lineage Clearing on that side.

Again, I refer to my sister Julie's heart attack at 43. Julie was doing some tremendous healing work at the time. She is a powerful healer in her own right and decided to go deeply into her own healing process. About twenty years prior to this she had a tumor removed from the lining of her lungs.

At that time she was in a difficult marriage, did not have much education (which limited her career choices), cared for their two young children (which made it hard for her to leave her husband) and had no financial resources. She was now attempting to heal her heart of the old trauma. In the process, she triggered the genetic heart weakness.

After I did the Ancestral Lineage Clearing process and cleared the energy, Julie began to recover. The doctors found a medication that thinned her blood without a severe allergic reaction and worked with her to control her cholesterol without drugs.

I would not have tried Ancestral Lineage Clearing while Julie's heart was overstressed or while my brother was recovering from his stint surgery. The release and the shifting of energy may have caused too much of a strain on their already damaged hearts. **It is extremely important to be sensitive to a present medical condition before proceeding on an energetic level.**

Other chronic dis-eases can be passed from generation to generation, affecting children through lifestyle, emotional influences, DNA and environmental factors. These can be addressed and removed on an energetic level by Ancestral Lineage Clearing. **Such dis-eases must always be in a stable medical condition before Ancestral Lineage Clearing is attempted.**

During the last several decades, Western medicine has recognized that addictions to alcohol, drugs, sex and food are dis-eases. Most are physical, some psychological and, from my perspective, all dis-eases are energetic related.

The physical needs of the body **under addictive influences** need to be addressed first. Emotional support is absolutely necessary, and behavioral changes must be learned over an extended period of time. Unless you are an addiction professional, do not attempt addiction relief through Ancestral Lineage Clearing. **Ancestral Lineage Clearing will NOT stop the addictive behavior. It is just one resource** to use in addressing addictive challenges; it is a powerful tool, but only one of a variety of resources. Addictions can be addressed on the energetic level by Ancestral Lineage Clearing after the physical and psychological addictions have been dealt with.

Moreover, if addiction is part of the family lineage, clearing it from your family line may be the greatest gift you could ever give them. No one wants their children affected by chronic conditions or addictions.

4. **Plateaus**

There are times in our lives when everything is running smoothly and no crisis looms, and yet there is restlessness, a sense of *something* waiting, *something* more *out there*, and *something* more to do or to be. This is a plateau; a level or holding place, a place of rest where we can reassess our life before we move on to the next stage of development. This is a significant time for exploration of possibilities.

It can also be a time of impatience, depression, anxiety or helplessness. If we can rest in this place and wait for resolution, life will supply the answers. There are times, however, when questing for deeper answers becomes important. Ancestral Lineage Clearing can also assist us in finding answers to pressing questions of which we are not yet aware.

When a client comes at this stage in life, identifying an issue may be difficult because there is no precise problem or challenge. Consequently, looking for a specific ancestor with the particular problem is not an effective approach.

At these times, I take the client into the meditation to move into the past time stream to search for the lifetime, or ancestor, who will give the client the most valuable information and understanding needed at this time. This is most successful.

Once when I was at a plateau in my business and didn't know whether to alter my business plan or to continue on course, an Ancestral Lineage Clearing helped me gain clarity.

Integrity

I saw an ancestor was overlooking the desert from a tower or the top floor of a multi-story building. From her perspective, the people looked small and far away, in what appeared to be Egypt or some other Middle Eastern country. This ancestor was obviously wealthy, dressed in beautiful clothes, had an elaborate hairstyle and was surrounded by servants to do her bidding.

She was the widow of a successful merchant, and since his death she had taken over his business. She wanted to take her place in the merchant trade and gain the respect of the tradesmen in the area, for she was intelligent and shrewd. But this woman had no friends, nor a mentor to guide her in the transition.

The widow had become involved in a border dispute with a neighbor over a piece of valuable land. She had used her wealth and power to manipulate the officials of the government to obtain title to the disputed land.

Everyone knew how she had unfairly managed to get the title away from the neighbor. Now her late husband's tradesmen treated her as an opponent, driving hard bargains and not giving her the pricing or trade favors her husband had relied on for years to make the business profitable. With everyone treating her so harshly, she became bitter and resentful. She thought she had to be tough and unyielding, and so she was.

My ancestor had the reputation of being the least favorite trader to deal with because of her attitude and temper. She struggled with the business until it eventually failed. When she died she was poor, alone and disliked.

When I asked her to go to the *Choice Point*, she was more than willing to do so.

She went back to the time after her husband's death when the land dispute arose. Instead of choosing to influence the officials to give her title to the land, she chose to go to her neighbor and discuss the land dispute with him. They worked out a compromise to use the land and meet their respective needs, and made a deed that reflected both of their interests.

Since she successfully negotiated the land dispute, she felt more confident in dealing with other traders who knew she had dealt fairly with her neighbor. The traders were now willing to trade fairly with her.

The business continued to prosper and she made many good friends throughout her life. She was known to be fair and honest in her dealings.

When my ancestor died, she was a respected member of the community and greatly beloved because of her charities and good works.

This lifetime told me of potential future strife, perhaps in being tempted to manipulate a situation unfairly to my advantage. If I stay true to myself and act for the mutual good of all parties, not only will the disagreement be resolved but it will reflect positively on future business dealings.

There was no indication now that I need to change the business. However, it is important for me to pay attention to how I conduct business with everyone, because my actions reflect on my reputation. This was a good lifetime to explore for advice on maintaining integrity in my business.

Conclusion

Ancestral Lineage Clearing is beneficial in a variety of situations to assist people in releasing energy from their family heritage. Inherited lifetimes patterns and negative behaviors can be energetically addressed and shifted sometimes in a single session.

The greatest benefit of Ancestral Lineage Clearing is that this change can permanently affect the person's energy field and the energy pattern in other living family members—and, in the generations to come. It is a powerful and dynamic healing tool.

PART II
The Healing Process

Chapter IX
Identifying the Issue and Setting the Intention

What is a **Family Pattern**? What family wound or pattern do you want to release in your life?

We look for help in life when we feel that *something* is missing. Perhaps we are making repeated mistakes or there is something else wrong. Sometimes it is obvious, like lack of money, or subtle, like lack of self-esteem. How does one identify an issue or pattern in life that needs to be cleared?

When we seek help, we usually have an idea about the basic challenge or challenges we are facing. But, we may not be able to pinpoint the exact challenge or what we want to work on first.

Step 1 is to determine the most troublesome issue in your life. If you don't know which issue is most challenging for you, then you must first decide what topic most overwhelms you. Which problem takes the most time, effort, attention, worry and energy? Life's challenges generally fall within the following categories:

- Family
- Relationships
- Work or career

139

- Money or finances
- Spiritual or religious matters
- Health

List all the challenges, difficulties or problems you see in your life. Use another sheet of paper if you need additional space.

_____

_____

_____

_____

_____

Then, prioritize and pick the most important issue. Is your failing relationship (or, lack of a relationship) the most important challenge in your life, or is it the lack of money? Number them in order of importance, beginning with the most important subject. You can rearrange the list several times until you are satisfied with it.

Step 2 is to look at your family members and see if any of them have the same or a similar challenge in his/her life.

For example, if you cannot manage to sustain an important relationship in your life, do you have an aunt or uncle who has been divorced four or five times, or one who, by the age of 50, has never been married? Or, a relative who was only married for five years, and 25 years later still desires a relationship? Write down the names of these relatives.

_____   _____

_____   _____

_____   _____

_____   _____

_____   _____

Is there a family pattern here, or are you the only one with this issue? Be sure to distinguish **whether you are the only one dealing with the issue, or if you are simply the only one talking about it.** In many families, silence and secrets remain an accepted manner of dealing with difficult problems. However, if you are the only one with this issue, then perhaps another mode of healing or handling the issue may be more effective (i.e., psychological therapy, past life regression or soul retrieval).

What if you are adopted, or don't know your relatives? I recommend you just sit quietly and see if you can feel intuitively whether or not this is only your personal concern, or an issue from the deep family past. Even if you do not know your heritage, you will have a sense of whether something is deeply rooted in the past, or is a close, present challenge. If you meditate, I suggest you meditate and seek an answer from the stillness. Is your challenge from your birth family or your foster/adoptive family, and if so, which parent? Your meditation will point the way.

Step 3 **is to decide from which side of the family this question is most closely derived**. Is it your mother's side of the family that has the challenge of self-esteem? Are your aunts, uncles and cousins on the maternal side either blow-hards or shy and self-effacing? Or are they on your father's side of the family – the ones who cannot keep jobs, or those who are workaholics and neglect their families for career's sake? **Review your primary challenge and determine if you seek an ancestor from your maternal or paternal side of the family**.

Maternal Side   Paternal Side

_____   _____

_____   _____

_____   _____

_____   _____

Sometimes it is not clear which side of the family the challenge comes from. Review Step 2 and see if there are more relatives from one side of the family or the other. This may be your first clue.

Another indication of the relevant side of the family may be if one side of the family has had more difficulty with the issue than the other. For example, let's say the challenge is one of maintaining relationships. If Uncle Johnny (on Dad's side) has had five wives, but he's the only one with this extreme problem, then it may just be Uncle Johnny's personality. If all of Mom's brothers and sisters have been divorced and some have been divorced at least two or three times, then this may really be a maternal issue.

It is important to identify whether or not the pattern is from the maternal or paternal line. When we search for the specific ancestor who set the pattern in the family, we need to know which lineage to follow. If you plan to travel to either to California or Florida you will end up in a very different place, depending upon the route you choose.

Always follow your intuition and instincts when you determine from which side of the family an issue arises. Numbers may indicate it is your father's side, but depth of challenge may incline you toward your mother's side of the family. I find that every client has an intuitive *knowing* from which side of the family the issue has come.

Occasionally, a client will find that a pattern that comes through strongly on both sides of the family. I found this was true on the poverty issues in my family, but for different reasons. In such cases it may be necessary to do two Ancestral Lineage Clearings separately in order to clear the family patterns in both sides of the family. Since we cannot go in two directions at once, we need to first visit one family, and then visit the other side of the family.

Step 4 is to refine the issue to its core elements. Write down all of your **limiting beliefs** about this challenge, including your **feelings**. Use another sheet if you need additional space.

_____   _____

_____   _____

_____   _____

_____   _____

Now refine the subject matter of the challenge into its smallest or basic part. If you get to the point where you feel tears welling up within you, feel your throat closing up or begin to cry, you are getting close to, or have reached the core issue.

For example, money is a big challenge for many of us in America's consumer society; however, money itself is NEVER the core issue. Money is just a piece of paper and some metal. So let me go through this process of refining the subject to reach the core issue.

Limiting beliefs about money:
I don't deserve money
Money always slips through my fingers
Money is power
I have to hang on to this terrible job or I'll never have enough money to pay my bills
No one will love me unless I have money
I don't want to worry about money
I resent rich people
I have to work hard for money
I never have enough money for my needs
Money is security
No one will respect me without money
I lost my job, so now I'm a loser
There is not enough money in the world for everyone's needs.

As you can see, there are many different issues around money. Our views of money in this culture have to do with self-esteem, work, security, love, social values, power, respect and judgment. These kinds of challenges also arise in other areas of our lives, such as love, careers, families and spirituality. The more you explore the details of the issue, the closer you can move toward the core of what you are seeking from your particular ancestor.

There are different methods for finding your essential core issue if you cannot discover it by writing down all your beliefs.

One valuable technique is to draw a spiral on a piece of paper. Start small, and make it as large as the paper will hold. Set your intent to find the core belief that is holding you back. Then, at the outside of the large end of the spiral, begin to write your limiting beliefs. Write small so that you can include several beliefs before you reach the center. As you move toward the center of the spiral, you will go deeper and deeper into the root of your belief system until you reach the core.

Another powerful method for reaching your core belief is to set your intention and go into a meditation, seeking the essential belief that is holding you back from finding your freedom in this area. Begin by entering into a meditative state as you would normally. If you do not have a regular meditation routine, there are several available to download from the web, or you can purchase CDs or take classes. You can also enter a deep meditative state by following your breath as it moves slowly in and out of your body, releasing your thoughts until you reach the stillness.

When you are in the meditative or alpha stage, state your intention to discover the core limiting belief of your challenge. Hold a peaceful state of mind, without judgment, that this belief is in your life. Let all extraneous thoughts go by. If limiting beliefs show up, let them come. Follow them to other limiting beliefs until you feel, sense, hear or *know* that you have reached the core. When you have the intuitive knowing that *this* belief—these words or feelings are the ones you have been searching for—then you know you are complete.

When you are ready to slowly come out of the meditation, breathe deeply breathe deeply three times. Begin to sense the world around you, feel the space around your body and the sensations within your body. Begin to move, stretch, and come back to this time and place. I recommend writing down the insights you received in the meditation, as many people forget what they learned once they become fully awake again.

Step 5 is to define your challenge and make a clear intention of seeking the ancestor who initiated the issue in your heritage. If we go looking for the ancestor who caused the "problems in our family," we may meet every ancestor in every past generation. We probably all inadvertently cause our loved ones problems! However, **we are looking for one specific ancestor at a time for a particular issue, and** we need to focus on the one we are seeking.

Once we have identified the core issue, then we can **construct a clear intention to** seek the correct ancestor. In the example above, we defined the core issue as having to do with lack of money. But, let's say the core issue is 'security.' When we begin our search, we will state an intention "to search for our ancestor who lacked security in his or her life, and wanted money to satisfy that need."

Or, if the core issue were the inability to maintain a long-term relationship due to a lack of trust, then we would begin our search with the intention "to search for our first ancestor whose trust was broken in their long-term relationship."

It is important to frame the intention in neutral or blame-free terms in order to discover your ancestor and acquire his or her help. If we seek an ancestor "who is the SOB that started the abuse cycle in the family," we may find him or her, but they may not be in a particularly helpful mood. One of my clients recently searched for the ancestor who started the sexual abuse in her family. Since this request occurred in a group setting, I did not have the opportunity to individually counsel each person before the search. When the woman located her ancestor, he had his back turned toward her and she could not get any further in the session. We reframed the issue to look for her ancestor *who had challenges relating to women sexually and felt powerless.* This resulted in a more successful outcome.

Another client had difficulty clearing a money issue until we rephrased the issue in neutral terms without any blame attached. He then searched for his ancestor *who had difficulties holding onto the money he had.* This resulted in a clearing of the energy surrounding his money issue.

Though this may seem difficult, try to approach setting the intention statement from the ancestor's point of view. In the case of my ancestor who started the heart dis-ease in the family, he did not intend for his descendants to continue to die of heart dis-ease. To seek his help, I looked for an ancestor *who first had physical and emotional issues with the heart that resulted in heart difficulties.* As a child, the ancestor who began the sexual abuse did not begin his life thinking about how to sexually abuse women. Some incident or circumstance drove him to that first abuse.

Money difficulties are common. These issues sometimes get set in the DNA from our ancestors who were slaves and never had money, or from wealthy relatives who never had to earn or manage money. Many negative family patterns result from traumatic circumstances with which the ancestor was unable to cope during his or her lifetime. (For an example read the story, *Slavery and Survival* in Chapter VIII.) An emotional reaction was formed by these traumatic events and, when this emotional trauma could not be cleared or released, it became set in the family genetics.

Therefore, carefully frame the intention statement to search for your ancestor in neutral terms that define the core issue in your life. **Realize that your ancestors did not intentionally set out to cause harm to themselves or others, but difficulties may have resulted from their words, thoughts or actions, which they could not have**

predicted. Your intentions to heal will clear and release the unintended result of your ancestor's actions. Your ancestor wants to heal his or her own life and, therefore, also the lives of future generations.

Once we have identified the challenge, determined the side of the family from which it arose, refined the challenge to its central core issue and formed the intention statement, we are ready to move on to the actual search for the ancestor.

To summarize: Before beginning the journey to seek the ancestor:

1. Define the issue: is it a family pattern?
2. Determine the proper side of the family.
3. Refine the underlying core issue.
4. Set a clear intention.
5. Define the intention in neutral terms.

When the intention is properly set the ancestor will draw you to him- or herself to clear the pattern.

Conclusion

A successful release and clearing of the present day challenge (in your life, or in the life of your client) relies on preliminary preparations. By getting to the core issue and asking the correct question, your ancestor will willingly appear to help you or your client out of your present challenge.

Preparations:

1. Define the issue.
2. Determine whether or not it is a family pattern suitable for Ancestral Lineage Clearing.
3. Create the intention statement.

Chapter X
Beginning the Healing and Clearing Process

Introduction for Use of Ancestral Lineage Clearing

Now that you understand the theory behind Ancestral Lineage Clearing, the following chapters will take you through the actual process. There are three ways in which to reset a family pattern using the method in this book.

1. **DO NOT ATTEMPT TO DO AN ANCESTRAL LINEAGE CLEARING ALONE THE FIRST TIME. Even after many years, most people who do energetic healing of any kind have a partner, friend or colleague holding sacred healing space for them while doing a healing process, including me.**

2. I strongly recommend that you can seek professional assistance with the clearing the first time – or any time you feel uncertain or that you may need assistance.

3. You can ask a friend or healing colleague to share this experience with you in exchange for one of their services. Exchange is ideal for healers, energy workers or experienced journey workers.

All methods are possible and effective. Here are some considerations to help you determine which method is best for you.

If you have considerable self-awareness, are a healer, have done emotional processing work for three or more years, **and** you meditate regularly, you should have no difficulty clearing negative family patterns with someone holding the healing, sacred space for you. Clearing and releasing is standard emotional processing practice. If you can do extended journey work during deep meditation and return safely, then you should be comfortable following the instructions and seeking your ancestor. **If you have any doubts, do the initial clearing with a certified professional.**

If you are not experienced in healing or meditation, and have not experienced multiple meditation journeys, it may be challenging to come out of the meditation and ground or center yourself after the meditation. It is sometimes tempting to remain in the past visiting other ancestors, and one can lose track of time and space. Many beginners become so engrossed they do not want to come back home timely. **No one should do more than one journey at a time without extensive experience.**

A professional energy worker or certified Ancestral Lineage Clearing specialist can keep track of the details regarding the next step. For instance, this person can help you find your core issue, guide the meditation, ask questions during the meeting with your ancestor, bring you out of the meditation, release the energy and reset new energy.

The professional can ensure that you are fully grounded in your body and have integrated the new energy *before* you move on to the stage of setting the new energy. The best support a healer can give is to hold safe space for you while you explore and fully enter into this process. The website http://*www.AncestralLineageClearing.com* can give you resources for contacting me or another certified practioner for a session.

Even after doing this process myself for eight years, as well as working with clients and teaching it, I ask a healer friend to be with me when I am challenged rather than attempting to hold the energy myself.

The dangers of attempting to heal a family pattern using this technique without a proper background are potentially significant, depending on your health and the issue you are dealing with. I want everyone to proceed with caution.

If you come back too rapidly from a meditative state or a journey, you might experience headache, nausea, disorientation, a floating sensation, an inability to feel your body, ungrounded, confusion, emotional instability and perhaps other physical and emotional sensations not listed here. It may be a bit like jumping off a high swing while still in mid-air. These symptoms can be avoided by slowly and deliberately easing into breathing and movement.

If toning or sounding continues too long, some people experience agitation, ringing in the ears, irritation and skin tingling. Pay attention to your body and the sensations you are experiencing, and you will know when to stop the toning and sound; however, knowledge and experience are required in order to sense when to turn off the toning and sound before discomfort occurs. These unpleasant sensations generally do not last long but this healing is supposed to be a positive experience. If done with consciousness and care, it usually is.

The best option for your first experience is to seek professional assistance from a certified practioner of Ancestral Lineage Clearing for Healing a Family Pattern. The assistance of a certified Ancestral Lineage Clearing specialist is helpful if:

a. You are not familiar with energy healing or meditation;

b. This is your first experience delving into the metaphysical world of self-healing;

c. There is a traumatic or deep-seated emotional family issue you wish to face;

d. You are having challenges identifying the core issue after several attempts, particularly in painful areas such as chronic illnesses, long-term issues and deep dissatisfaction;

e. You have tried to locate your ancestor and have been unable to do so, or you are unable to follow the ancestor's life;

f. The ancestor is uncertain or confused at the choice point;

g. You cannot intuitively receive the affirmations or guidance to reset the new energy in your field.

Having a professional hold **safe space** is invaluable in order for you to let go of doubts, fears and apprehensions as you seek the ancestor who will aid you in altering your core issue.

"Safe space" is a term for a confidential setting in which one person offers to hold another in a physically, emotionally, mentally and spiritually protected place. It is important to the process for you to be totally open and free with thoughts, words and actions, without fear of judgment or repercussion. Safe space often becomes sacred space when prayers and the protection of the Divine or guardian spirits are invoked. Once a person can safely express doubts, fears and apprehensions while on this journey, the process will operate on its own despite the person's fears.

Bob was a client with very strong abandonment issues. He did very well in meeting his ancestor and following the first life. I discussed his session in the *Abandonment* story in Chapter VII. When the time came to allow his ancestor to go to the *Choice Point,* the client wanted to control the ancestor with his own mental image of what the *Client would do*, rather than allowing the ancestor to choose his destiny.

We stopped the session and I gave the client some exercises to do to change *his mental preconceptions.* The first exercise cleared his energy field again, and helped him to relax and trust the process. Deep breathing, going deeper into the meditation and letting go of the ego control, helped him back into the observer position. When he let go of his need to control the past, the ancestor immediately did what he needed to do, and the abandonment issue was resolved.

Sometimes the ancestor is confused about how to find the Choice Point earlier in his or her own life. The ancestor is so caught up in the trauma of that life that it is difficult to choose a deciding point that will truly make a difference. I discussed an ancestor who encountered this struggle in the *Control Issue* story in Chapter VII.

If you become confused while attempting to clear negative family patterns, a Certified Ancestral Lineage Clearing practioner can show you how it works. Knowing where your resistance appears can be beneficial. The website http://*www.AncestralLineageClearing.com* can give you resources for reaching me or another certified practioner.

Other nuances may occasionally arise during a session where only experience or intuition can help. I have frequently had clients who were met at the time stream by guides or spirit helpers who led the way to ancestors. These spirits were not ancestors themselves, nor were they guides familiar to the clients beforehand. I had to decide at the time whether these spirits were there to aid or to interfere in the process. Because of my familiarity with the process, I knew what to do. These unexpected situations can interfere with a novice's clearing process.

Preparation—Clearing the Space

Before you begin an Ancestral Lineage Clearing Session, I recommend that you first clear the space you will be using. If you are doing an Ancestral Lineage Clearing session for someone else, be sure to clear your own energy field, too. *Clearing space* means clearing out the old energy and leaving a positive or neutral space for the energy work.

When you prepare to heal a family pattern, you do not want to deal with any other energy, such as an argument you may have had with your brother, the baby crying, the wild action movie you watched, or any other life complications. In order for the healing process to be effective, you basically want a clean slate.

There are many different ways to energetically clear and cleanse space of negative energy. I will list only the most common and easiest methods here. If you regularly cleanse your space, please utilize whatever skills and methods you are comfortable with.

1. One of the most common methods is called **smudging.** It is a Native American practice of burning dried sage leaves in a bowl (or a smudge stick) until they are smoking. Once the sage leaves are lit, blow out the actual fire and allow the leaves to smoke. Use a feather to wave the smoke over objects or people to clear and purify their energy, both front and back. You may also use a combination of sage and cedar.

The sage and cedar are for purification and cleansing. The smoke takes the prayers up to the Great Spirit in the sky. While you are scattering the smoke, pray for purification and blessing on the place. You will smudge all who enter the sacred space.

2. Another clearing ceremony uses a mix of salt water spray. **Salt water**, like the ocean, **clears negative energy** and deposits negative ions (these are good ions) into the air. The salt water washes away energy that resides in the place you are using and leaves a neutral space for new energy.

To use salt water for clearing: Mix about one teaspoon of sea salt per cup of water and put in spray bottle or bowl. Spray or sprinkle the mixture around the area where the ceremony will be held. Be careful not to spray the water where it will spot. Salt water will stain silk, and water-spot rayon, so be careful around fragile fabrics. Be careful not to get this mixture near your eyes.

As you spray the salt water, set your intentions for a positive outcome and good healing experience. If you have a spiritual orientation, this is the time to say a prayer, call in the Creator, and invoke your angels, guardians, and good spirits, God, Goddess or the Divine. Ask for assistance, clarity, ease of contact, support for yourself and your ancestor, or whatever you need at the moment. In the next section I have copied a beautiful prayer that feels perfect for this setting.

3. In phone sessions, I often use **sound energy** to cleanse an environment. Sound waves carry powerful energy to clear, cleanse, heal and transform. Melodious and harmonic sounds generally heal; dissonant and disharmonic sounds cleanse and release energy.

You can use either an instrument or your voice to clear energy with sound. If you have a drum or rattle, or any sort of instrument, merely begin a dissonant or unharmonious sound, with no rhythm or harmony. The worse it sounds the more effective it will be in breaking up the energy in the room. Continue for several minutes, then stop and check to see if the energy in the room has changed is clear. If it still feels flat, stale, smoky or sticky, continue with the sounds. You may find yourself falling into a harmony, but do not be concerned; simply let it go and return to disharmony. We are all conditioned to make pretty sounds, and this is one time when we don't want to do that.

While you are sounding the dissonant notes, set your intentions to clear and cleanse yourself, the client and the space of negative energy, and transform the energy to neutral and positive energy for the ceremony. Then, set your intentions for a positive outcome and a good experience.

Exercise: Practice using one of the cleansing and purifying exercises above in your own space. Feel the difference in the energy in the room before and after the cleansing.

The Altar

Some people use an altar in Ancestral Lineage Clearing, and some do not. This is a personal preference. I use one for two reasons.

First, an altar gives both the client and me a focal point. The altar is a place to focus our prayers, the intentions, the core issue, the family dynamics and the helpful energy.

The altar consists of whatever you consider beneficial to the process. My altar usually contains representations of the four basic elements: fire, water, wind and earth. I always meditate on what my

159

client needs in advance, and I have crystals on my altar to assist both my client and me. I ask the client to bring in photos of the maternal or paternal side of the family that will be affected by the session and we place those on the altar as well.

If you have a particular religious affiliation you may want to place a cross, a Buddha, a picture, a symbol or an angel on the altar, to assist you on your journey. I had a client place a statue of the Virgin Mary on her altar when we dealt with issues around her mother.

I usually keep my rattles on the altar to *charge* them with the energy of the session, until reuse later for releasing and resetting the energy. Drums, rattles, gongs, bells, flutes or any other instruments should be on the altar or near at hand. Later in the ceremony you will want to use these instruments for clearing.

Second, an altar absorbs and holds the energy of the ceremony conducted in its presence. Sacred objects become imbued with power when used in ceremonies and the prayers that people invest in them. If you place an item on the altar, such as a picture of your family, with the intention of healing a family issue, the healing process will be imbedded in the picture itself for a certain period of time. If you continue to use the picture as a focal point while praying for your family, those prayers will continue to be carried to the family in the picture; and, the picture itself will carry the prayers if you give it away to someone else.

If you want to continue the healing of the Ancestral Lineage Clearing beyond the session on a stronger or more conscious level, bring a symbol, crystal, picture or other object to place on the altar that will carry the energy forward. It isn't necessary, but the object acts as a physical reminder of the ceremony's energetics.

If I am doing a session in person, I frequently ask the client to bring in an object or photo to place on the altar to help carry the session's energy. If it is a phone session, I will ask the client to set up an altar at home and place the special items on it.

Exercise: Create an altar for your Ancestral Lineage Clearing session. What did you place on it, and why?

The Ancestral Lineage Clearing Prayer

As I was writing this book, I discovered a lovely prayer which is from Ho'oponopono Pule, a Hawaiian spiritual tradition that fits perfectly with Ancestral Lineage Clearing. You might wish to start each session with this prayer. This is part of a longer prayer that Morrnah (the creator of Ho'oponopono Pule) is said to have helped heal hundreds, if not thousands, of people. It is simple, but powerful:

Divine creator, father, mother, son, daughter as one ...
If I, my family, relatives and ancestors have offended you, your family, relatives and ancestors in thoughts, words, deeds and actions from the beginning of our creation to the present, we ask your forgiveness...
Let this cleanse, purify, release, cut all

**the negative memories, blocks, energies
and vibrations and transmute these
unwanted energies to pure light ...And it
is done.**

You may want to say this as an opening and closing
prayer.

Prayer is personal between you and the
Divine, and I do not presume to dictate to anyone
how to pray. Say what is in your heart and the
Universal Spirit will hear you. For my prayer, I often
call in the four directions, along with my ancestors
and the client's ancestors, as well as our spirit guides
and angels, to guide us and support us on our sacred
journey.

Conclusion

Ancestral Lineage Clearing is a serious
healing technique and should be used with care and
consideration for your own health and the health of
your clients.

Proper preparation is essential to safe and
successful healing of a family pattern. Before you
begin, be sure to consider:

Will you perform this ceremony alone or with
assistance?

How will you cleanse the space?

Do you want to set up an altar?

What do you want to place on it?

Will you say an opening prayer, and what
will it be?

Chapter XI
Searching for the Ancestor

After identifying the issue and constructing the intention statement to locate the specific ancestor, the time has come to search for our ancestor. There are multiple steps in the search, and I will break them down into very specific parts so that they flow easily and quickly.

Before you begin the actual search process, read this section over completely. This should be an **uninterrupted process**, and can take between twenty minutes and an hour-and-a-half. Plan on the extended time with your first search, particularly if you are not familiar with meditation and journey work.

Step 1: Meditation or Relaxation Exercise.

Breathe deeply and move into a meditative state. If you know how to meditate, use your usual meditation practice to reach the still, quiet place within.

If you do not know how to meditate or have never done a relaxation exercise, choose a quiet place free from all distractions (TV, radio, pets, children, people, telephone, pager, cell phone, blackberry, iPhone). If there are other people in the house, let them know what you are doing or put a *do not disturb* sign on the door. Settle into a comfortable chair with your feet on the ground, in a place that is neither too hot nor cold. Many people find that their body temperature drops a little during meditation, so you may want to have a light blanket handy.

If you find it difficult to relax and meditate you may find that lying down works. If you tend to fall asleep, sit upright in a chair. You may have to practice several times to determine which works better for you.

Then, slowly breathe in deeply through your nose and, as you breathe out through your mouth, you may make a sound like *whoosh* or *whooo* as you release the cares of the day.

Take another slow, deep breath in through your nose, and let it out through your mouth, with or without sound, allowing the chatter of the mind to flow out with your breath.

Take a third slow, deep breath, in through your nose and out through your mouth, with or without sound, and be fully present in this moment of *now*.

Begin to breathe normally. Relax. Notice your body quieting down.

Relax your mind. Quiet all mind noise. If you notice any mind chatter, just let it pass by. Do not try to fight it, just let it go. Relax, relax, relax.

Step 2: Beginning the Journey.

We will now go on a journey. If you already know how to journey, you may skip to **The Journey.** If you are not familiar with journeying, then let me explain and give you some tips.

Everyone has a **primary mode for taking in, or absorbing information**. Most people take in information visually, which is why we like movies, and why advertising is so heavily visual. If you read and make pictures in your head, then you are a visual person. If someone tells you a story and you can see the story in your mind, you are probably a **visual person**.

Not all people are visual. Many people are **auditory:** musicians, for instance, or people who listen to tapes and learn by hearing. Auditory people recognize people by their voices, remember bits of music and song, what people said, the words in a movie and sounds of nature, etc.

Then there are **tactile folks** who like to feel the world. Remember the kids who squirmed in school when writing? Those were the tactile ones. Athletes are generally tactile, great with their body in motion. These are people who need to feel objects like wood, flowers, silk, skin, metal, etc. They feel experiences.

What do all these styles tell you? They tell you that **you will respond differently to journeying**, depending upon whether you are a visual, auditory or tactile person. You need to find what works best for you in order to make your journey the most powerful experience. If I say "step into the stream," you may visualize stepping into the stream, you may hear me say the words and hear the water splashing around your feet, or you may feel the cool/warm water covering your feet and rising up your legs. All of these experiences are valid. The deeper you move into the experience of the journey, the more quickly and deeply you will connect with your ancestor and the energy patterns.

If you are a healer and will be taking clients on journeys, then it is important you know whether they are visual, auditory or tactile. If you forget to ask, make sure you give enough information in the meditation and journey for all sensory types, so everyone will experience the necessary sensations.

Despite the fact that we may be primarily orientated to one sense, all of us relate to *all* senses. It is a good practice to fill the journey with multiple sensory images.

Total Safety on the Journey

You or your client will be going to usual and unusual places, possibly having strong reactions to where you go. Even if you are afraid or are going to some scary place, *you will have total control over what you experience in the journey*. Let me explain:

For instance, I will take you to a stream of water and ask you to lie down in it. If you are afraid of water you may panic. *Do not panic. You have total control.* If you do not want to lie down in the water, visualize (say or feel) a boat, raft, or other floating device that will make you feel safe.

Remember that you or your clients are actually in a chair and you will not drown. We don't want you to drown in the journey either. You have the power to make yourself feel safe on the journey.

On the other hand, if your issue is fear of flying and you encounter your ancestor flying an airplane in WWI, you don't want him to be on the ground. Something in the experience of flying is necessary for you to learn in order to clear the fear of flying from the family pattern.

You can, however, visualize wearing a parachute, a helmet, an impregnable flying suit, or feel as if you are watching from outside the plane, maybe like an angel, or any number of other scenarios.

In other words, you can construct a safe journey without affecting the situation you are viewing, hearing or feeling. So just continue to breathe normally, feeling relaxed, comfortable and safe.

Step 3: The Journey.

Begin by visualizing, hearing, feeling and sensing yourself in the midst of a meadow on a lovely warm spring day.

The sun is warm and shining, a breeze is blowing across your cheek, the temperature is perfect, there are wildflowers in the meadow, and you can hear birds singing. You notice trees to one side, and you walk over and discover a path into a forest.

The cool shade draws you in as you hear water flowing. You follow the sound and the pathway until you come to a beautiful shining stream with two currents. This is the **Time Stream.** One current flows into the past and the other flows into the future.

You sit at the base of a tree by the stream and remove your shoes and socks. [*This is an important focal point in the journey. The placement of the shoes and socks represents **an anchor point in time and space.** When you or the client comes back in time, the shoes and socks at the base of this tree will let you or the client know you are back in the present time and space.*]

As you step into the clear water, **you set your intention to find the ancestor who originated the issue you want resolved in your life.** You lie down in the current running back in time and relax, knowing it will take you to the exact time and place you need to go.

As you lay in the stream the water gently begins to move. You have a sense about whether you will be going into the recent past, or whether your ancestor lived in a time far away.

The current picks up speed. You hear the water rushing past your ears and the trees moving on the shore as your body is carried downstream. Wait patiently until the current begins to slow down and moves you to the shore.

Stand up and give a little shake. You are automatically dry.

Step 4: Contacting your Ancestor.

Step onto the shore and move into the landscape.
What do you see? Keep moving until you identify buildings, farms, shelters, people, or an action taking place.

Now what do you see, hear, smell, taste and feel? What are the clothing, shoes, animals, buildings, tools or vehicles like? Do you know what place or time period you are in? Does it matter?

Soon you will see or feel someone doing or saying something. Do not try to push this. You will naturally be drawn in a direction and to a person.

Open up your mind and heart to this person. What is s/he doing or saying? What do you know about him/her?

Then just observe the action. Who is interacting with this person? What action or inaction is this person taking? What is the situation?

Ask questions and see if you *know* the answers. You do not have to actually ask the ancestor.

This is similar to contacting a person on a street and knowing that he is a fisherman by the clothes he is wearing, how he smells, the condition of his hands and his accent.

Generally, the first person you identify is the ancestor. Or, it could be that your ancestor is the first person this original person meets. Just wait and watch. Sense what you are feeling.

You have made contact, and this observation gives you the context for your ancestor. If you wait, watch and feel, you will discover who they are, how they arrived at that point in their life, what they are feeling and what they intend to do with their life.

For example, in Steve's clearing (in the story *Misunderstood* in Chapter VIII) he first found his ancestor chopping wood alone in the forest. By watching and opening up to the presence of this man, Steve could tell he was bringing the wood to his home in the forest where his wife and children waited. He lived away from a community in an isolated home without friends or family nearby. He felt like a failure.

Then, if you are doing the session, you can inquire further. Why does he feel like a failure? Why does he live in isolation? Where is he from?

When you ask, you will receive responses as if the ancestor were thinking about things in his past, or you will just **know** the answers.

You can also move back and forth through time as if you could fast forward or replay the

person's life. If you did not get an answer to the question of where he is from and why he is living here, then just move back in time several years and observe what was happening in that time period to see what led up to this moment.

When you let yourself be guided, you will instinctively go to the right time and place to find the answers.

After you understand what is happening in your ancestor's life, **consider how it affects the question or intention for which you went into the past.** Do you know why you cannot handle money, based on where this ancestor is and how he made his choices? If not, then the next step is to move forward in time and see what happens in the ancestor's life from this time forward.

As you observe the current situation, you will usually see the crisis point (or the result of that point) in the person's life. If it occurred much earlier in his/her life, you may not see it at this point.

Once you have identified and understood the ancestor's life path, continue to move through the ancestor's life in large increments of 20-30 year spans, until you reach the ancestor's deathbed. Observe how the ancestor died. Was s/he at home with loved ones, or alone? Did he die in battle or while hunting? Was s/he happy or sad, loved or disappointed, unfulfilled, dissatisfied, bored or neglected? **How did s/he feel about the way they lived their lives?**

Step 5: Asking the Ancestor to Change: i.e., the *Choice Point.*

Ask your ancestor if s/he would like to change life for the better and to change this pattern for their descendants. **All of the ancestors I have ever asked have said yes.**

At this point, very gently ask your ancestor to go to the *Choice Point* of his/her life, where they could have made a different choice, changing their life and taking them on a different path. Give your ancestor a moment to find the choice point in their life. They know where it is.

It may be the moment just before the crisis point where he got into the fight that ended in a death. It may have been years before in a childhood incident where she did not take care of her baby sister, and perhaps she has carried the guilt ever since.

Step 6: The New Energy

When the ancestor is at the *Choice Point*, ask him/her to make a different choice this time. The ancestor will. They know the outcome of the old choice and they *want* to change, so they will make a new choice.

Then follow the ancestor through their life after they make the new choice. See, feel, hear and watch how their new life unfolds and how the new opportunities for love, work, growth, community and fulfillment come into their life.

Pay particular attention to *your issue* and see if it even arises in the ancestor's lifetime. Finally, view the ancestor on their deathbed, and ask how they felt about how their life turned out.

You will find the ancestor's life will have altered dramatically. Their life will be happy, fulfilled and fruitful. The ancestor will have received what they wanted from life, and will have died happy on his/her deathbed. Remember this feeling and energy.

Step 7: Coming Back

After visiting the ancestor's deathbed, **thank your ancestor for having the courage and willingness to change their life.** Then walk back to the Time Stream and **step into the current that moves forward into the present, with the intention to take you home**.

Lie down in the current which leads forward in time, and relax. As you lay in the stream the water gently begins to move. The current picks up speed, and you hear the water rushing past your ears. The plants or trees move on the shore as your body is carried upstream. Wait patiently until the current begins to slow down and moves you to the shore.

Stand up and give a little shake. You are automatically dry. There, at the base of the tree, are your shoes and socks. You are home.

Step 8: Withdrawing from the Meditation

It is very important that you withdraw slowly and properly from a meditation. When you are deeply into a journey, your brain is in an alpha state, which is a different frequency than when you are awake. An abrupt awakening can cause physical distress such as dizziness, nausea, light-headedness, and inability to think or operate machinery, such as a car.

When you are back at the tree, put on your socks and shoes. Then stand up and walk back to the beautiful meadow. Begin by taking three deep breaths. Then breathe normally. Do not hyperventilate. Count slowly backwards from ten to one, telling yourself that when you reach one you will be fully and completely awake.

10 you are slowly coming awake.

9 you are becoming more aware

8 you are feeling better

7 you are breathing deeper

6 you can feel your hands and feet tingling

5 you can feel your head and arms tingling

4 you are feeling more awake

3 your full body is feeling awake

2 your mind is feeling active

1 you are completely and totally awake.

You should be fully awake when you reach the count of one. If you are still feeling fuzzy, walk around, drink some water and eat a snack. Then go on to the next phase of Releasing and Resetting the Family Pattern.

Conclusion

The meditation and journey to the ancestor is the heart of Ancestral Lineage Clearing. Our Ancestors want to aid us in having a happy and fulfilling life, and so they leap at the opportunity to change the life that brought about a distressing family pattern to their descendants. This journey changes lives forever.

Chapter XII
Releasing the Energy of the Negative Pattern

You have now taken the journey into the ancestor's past that initiated the life challenge, and we have observed, on a very personal, physical and energetic level, the anguish, pain and disappointment our ancestor felt in their life when they faced a critical event. We have now also felt the delight, happiness, satisfaction and peace that came when they made a positive choice for their life.

The purpose of resetting the Family Pattern is to clear the old dysfunctional pattern of the ancestor and reset the energy to the new positive pattern the ancestor found during our journey. The first step is to release the old energy pattern.

Releasing the Old Pattern

After returning from the journey you will still feel slightly relaxed from your meditation. It is important to stay in this relaxed state of mind.

Think of your challenge and of your ancestor's original life. Bring into your consciousness and into your physical body the feelings of the ancestor's original life energy. This is the energy that has remained *stuck* in the family DNA and carried down through the generations. This is the energy you will now release.

Connections to Mass Consciousness

In some situations, this ancestor, as well as the subject matter we will be releasing, may tap into a *mass consciousness* level. **When a traumatic event or circumstance affects certain groups of people or specific families, those circumstances may be locked into the psyche of the people who were emotionally, physically, mentally or spiritually linked or bound to one another by culture, village life, family ties or the traumatic event itself.**

For example, in the story *Slavery and Survival* in Chapter VIII of the village that was invaded by the North men who killed the men and enslaved all the women and children; the women and children were attached to each other by family genetic, emotional, tribal and religious ties. This created a group, or mass consciousness that was shared both before and after their enslavement.

By releasing the energy of this ancestor around depression, control and money, the client also released the energy for all those in the village who were attached or bonded during that lifetime (including their descendants). Only those people with whom the ancestor had familial, emotional, mental or spiritual attachments will be affected by the release and clearing of the energy.

If the challenge your ancestor meets is an individual one and does not involve a group of others, then no *mass consciousness* clearing is made. When Simon went back to find his farmer ancestor who moved into the woods and later returned to town and became a shoemaker, only his ancestor and the ancestor's family were involved. There was no group participation in that situation.

There are several methods to release negative energy.

1. Sound vibrations: I have discovered the most effective way to release negative energy is through sound.

Take an instrument such as a drum, rattle, bell or gong, and begin making disharmonious sounds or noise **to disrupt the energy field, with the intention to break up and release all negative energy** associated with this issue or subject, and all energy held by the ancestor in the original lifetime. If you don't have a musical instrument you can use your voice and make noises, called "toning," that are **dissonant and non-harmonious.** While I am using an instrument, I also use my voice to tone or make noises. It is definitely not singing. This is the same sounding that is used to clear and cleanse the area prior to setting the sacred space.

Disruptive noises are called dissonant sounds or sounds without rhythm, harmony or melody. **They are not supposed to be pleasant to the ear**. These sounds are supposed to disrupt all energetic fields and to break and shake loose all the negative energy that the client has been holding within their muscles, organs, cells and atoms.

The sounds will penetrate deeply within the body. Both the client and the healer should feel free to move, shake and shimmy. These dissonant sounds will break up the negative energy patterns that the client has been holding within his or her body, and in the DNA and chromosomes. Once the energy patterns are shaken loose and broken up into pieces they cannot harm anyone else.

The sound release should continue for at least one minute and perhaps three to five minutes, depending upon the depth and seriousness of the challenge and the length of time it has been in the family heritage. Both the healer's and client's bodies should be totally relaxed but energized when the negative pattern is released.

The healer/practitioner/client doing the sounding may want to stop and check periodically to find out where in the body the negativity is still holding. Is the client's neck tense? Does their stomach feel tight? Do they have a slight headache? Are their knees stiff? Is there any smoking, dark or strange energy hanging around anywhere in or around the body? Where are they still holding onto the past?

Both of you will know it is complete when you feel no tension or stress anywhere in your body.

If you continue sounding beyond the release point, the client may begin to experience pain. Your body may tighten and react negatively to the sound. It is important for you to **carefully monitor both of your reactions to the sounds.** When the sounds become physically irritating to me, I know that I've moved beyond the completion point.

When the negative energy is transformed and released, your body will feel relaxed, calm, energized and peaceful. Then, you will know to end the sounding.

Take a few deep breaths to calm your heart rate, and sit down to incorporate the new positive energy of your ancestor's new life and choice. Now you are ready to set the new energy into your energy bodies.

When I use sound with a client to release energy, I have them sit on a stool so that I can move all around them. I can reach over, under and around their arms, legs, head and torso. I check intuitively where energy is residing. I stop and ask them to check their body for places that feel tight and tense. When they tell me they are totally relaxed, and I feel it, too, I know the energy is released.

2. Visualization: If you and your client are visual people, another method of releasing is to visualize releasing the negative energy. If you have a regular meditation practice, this may be right for you.

Again, arrange both of you into a comfortable position, either in a chair or on a couch, in a sitting or lying down position. Begin to breathe in a slow and deliberate fashion until you feel relaxed.

Use your standard meditation practice, or continue breathing calmly and regularly as you bring in light from the top of your head down to your toes, touching every muscle and organ in the body until you are completely relaxed.

3. The Cleansing Meditation:

Imagine yourself in a beautiful green meadow with birds singing overhead, and with colorful wildflowers interspersed in the grass. You see a deer and her fawn in the distance. They move away and you begin to follow them. There is a path through the trees at the edge of the meadow where you follow the deer.

Soon you hear the sound of water. You come upon a clearing and see the deer drinking in a pond at the base of a small waterfall. You approach the pond and the deer move on,=unafraid, but keeping their distance. The pond feels cool in the warm air.

You know the waterfall is there just for you, to wash away all the negative energy from your ancestor's original lifetime and from dealing with this challenge during your prior life. The forest is quiet and you will not be disturbed. You go to the side of the waterfall and see a small nook where you take off your clothes, and step into the shallow pool.

Then you move under the waterfall, feeling its refreshing coolness. There are tiny champagne-like bubbles foaming around you. These bubbles clean, cleanse and release all the negative energy from your energy fields and your skin, and penetrate deeply within your body as they spread into the cellular levels of your DNA.

You know this flow is exactly what is needed to release and clear out the negative energy around your body.

The bubbles and the pool transform the negative energy into neutral or positive energy so that Mother Earth can use the energy for whatever She needs.

Stay under the waterfall for as long as you want. You will know when you are ready to leave when your body feels clear, clean and refreshed.

Check your body mentally and feel for any tension. If you feel tense or stiff anywhere, direct the water flow specifically to that place. Hold it there for a minute or two, then do a total wash down and recheck. It should take at least two to five minutes to clear and cleanse the negative family pattern.

When your whole body feels relaxed and refreshed, you know the energy is cleared and released.

Then step out of the waterfall, shake off and dry. Dress in the nook off the pond and retrace your steps to the meadow.

Follow the steps in the last chapter for coming slowly out of a deep meditation by counting down from ten to one.

4. Movement:

Another way of breaking up negative energy held in the body is to play music, and dance, shimmy, shake, jump up and down, crawl, slither and just move. **DO NOT THINK**. This exercise will work out the energy on a physical and energetic level without the intellectual effort of thinking, "I am releasing. I am releasing." Just allow it to happen, and it will.

Let your body tell you what it wants to do and how it wants to do it. Let go of whatever is in your head. Dance as if no one is looking. You are not trying to win a dance contest. This is about getting rid of negative energy.

If you want to scream and shout or make odd noises, go ahead. Do it! ☺ Listen to your body. Move it the way it wants to go. Does your body want to move slowly, up and down, side to side, rock, or move fast and furious?

Again, this will take some time. Let go for at least one to two minutes then do a body check. Is all the tension gone? Do you feel any stress in your body when you think of your core issues? Is your neck stiff, your head tight, your stomach in knots, or are your legs tense? If any part of you is still tense, keep moving until your total body feels free.

After checking your body for tension and tightness, you will know when you are free of the negative energy. Then, turn off the music, take a few deep breaths to calm your heart rate, and sit down to incorporate the new positive energy of your ancestor's renewed life and choice, as directed in the next chapter.

5. Combinations:

You may find it helpful to combine one or more of the above techniques. Doing movement while sounding and rattling or drumming is a natural combination to quickly shift energy.

Many people can visualize energy breaking up and washing away while rattling or drumming. Combining energy release modes easily and smoothly breaks up the negative energetic forces.

Conclusion

After you have released all the old negative energy of the core issue that came down through your lineage, it is now time to set the new, positive energy in your life and in your family's life. It is time to move on to the next chapter.

Chapter XIII
Setting the New Family Pattern

Now that the old energy pattern has been released, there is a vacuum in your energy field. How do you feel emotionally with this release – energized, empty, expectant? What do you feel in your body, mind and spirit? Are you aware of the space that the old energy occupied?

If this space is not promptly filled, the old energy will creep back in, as it is a familiar pattern. We've been comfortable with the old energetic presence; it has been around a long time, and other relatives are still feeling the pull of the old patterns.

It is now necessary to fill this void with the positive choice our ancestor made when given the second chance for their life.

As you sit back in your comfortable chair or relaxation place, recall the emotion of the ancestor in the second life. Remember the choices and the insights he or she discovered. Consider their happiness and joy when they decided to live with passion and love instead of despair, loneliness and failure.

Bring those emotions forward into your mind and heart. Feel them throughout your body. Think of how both you and your ancestor felt. Fill your spirit with the spark of love represented by a life well lived.

In order to retain these new energies in our own life, in our body, emotions, mind, and spirit, we must establish a new energetic practice for at least 27 days. Many psychological studies have told us that it takes 27-30 days to break an old habit and to establish a new one.

Simply because we have discovered the basis for the core family pattern doesn't necessarily mean that we can rely on the intellectual information alone to make positive change in our life. If we do not make the change, we will go right back to the way we have done things for the last 20, 30, 40 or 50 years. We know how to be miserable. We are successful at being unhappy. **Now is the time to choose *change.***

Step 1: Affirmations

When I intuitively ask Spirit how my client should establish the new energy, the first response I invariably receive is for the **client to do affirmations three times a day for 27 or 30 days.**

An **affirmation** is a positive statement or declaration of the truth that a desired goal is within reach. Affirmations are always positively stated in the present tense, dealing directly with the positive lesson learned and affirming the ability to create a new life with the new energy.

For example, with the client who was afraid to make decisions and choose a new life path (see Chapter IV for Kelsey's story, *Indecisiveness*, about the manager of the lumber mill), the affirmations went something like this:

> I am able to make good decisions that will create a positive outcome for all concerned.
> I am dependable and strong in my ability to decide the future and the future of all those who depend on me.

Spirit guides me in making all my decisions,
and I have confidence in my decisions.

The statements above meet all the criteria of good affirmations: a) positive statements, b) stated in the present tense, c) related to the positive aspects of the lesson of the core issue, and d) affirming her ability to create a new life with the new energy.

Another example is Steve's story of the farmer who lost his land and became a boot maker in *Misunderstood,* (see Chapter VIII). His affirmations were:

I am willing and able to ask for help when I need it.

I am strong and confident, and asking for help allows others to contribute to my success.

I am willing to help others, and by allowing others to help me I allow balance in my life.

It is always best to create your own affirmations, in your own words. I often suggest affirmations and strongly recommend the client use them for two or three days. The client is instructed to modify them after a few days, using their own words or ideas that come to them in meditations. You may add additional affirmations as you see fit.

Affirmations should be spoken out loud, though not necessarily in front of another person. You can speak them in front of a mirror, while driving, in bed when you first wake up or before you go to sleep, or anyplace that is convenient.

By speaking the affirmations aloud you are reinforcing the concepts through auditory and tactile senses, and, if you do them in front of a mirror, visually. Affirmations are very effective in modifying energy patterns.

Step 2: Objects to Hold Energy

I urge you to use your intuition to see what it tells you about other ways to set the energy in your field or in your client's field. These are suggestions based on the most common intuitive answers that I have received from Spirit.

Often the objects or pictures the client brings to a session can hold the new energy that is brought forward in the Ancestral Lineage Clearing Session. If the client has not brought an object to the session, something can be obtained later to hold the new energy.

There may be a specific object, or some type of article, that represents the new life energy of your ancestor. One of my clients was told to find a tiger to keep with her for 27 days. The tiger represented courage and determination in sticking to her path. She found a tiger emblem and put it on her windshield, to remind her that the tiger would aid in holding the energy she wanted to reinforce in life.

In other situations my clients have used an object to hold or carry in their pocket or purse, or to place on an altar or mantel as a daily reminder for 27 to 30 days.

These items can be crystals, boats, bridges, cats or bells. It makes no difference. The most important thing to remember is that you want to see and feel the object so that the memory of the ancestor's positive life energy is triggered. To reset the energy pattern, recall the energy in your body every time you see or feel the object. If you simply place a bell on a crowded mantelpiece and it becomes just another piece of junk, your eye merely skims over it, making it ineffective as a piece in which to reset the energy. Continually remind yourself *why* the bell is there.

How do you go about selecting a special item? The best method is to meditate or breathe deeply and listen to the still voice within you, and intuitively see or feel what object comes to you. If you are comfortable with meditation, this format will be familiar and easy to use.

Once I was on a phone session with a client, and there was no specific image in the journey that could be used as a power piece. Afterward, I searched and intuitively saw an image of a bridge. I thought this was odd because it was unrelated to the client's journey. However, I've found it useful to follow my guidance. When I told the client the vision I received to carry the new energy, he informed me that he was considering work to develop a new alloy to strengthen bridges. He was thrilled to receive this as his new energy object.

If you are not an experienced meditator you can use the following method: play some soft background music (without voices to distract you), sit quietly and begin breathing slowly. Concentrate on your breathing, in and out, and just let your thoughts pass through your mind without paying any attention to them. Just focus on your breathing.

When you feel calm and your body is relaxed and quiet, remember the positive energy of your ancestor's second life. Feel, hear, see and recall the energy that your ancestor felt when their life was happy and fulfilled.

Then, imagine, or ask your ancestor to give you, an image or object to hold the energy of this lifetime. DO NOT be in a hurry. Sit calmly and quietly while the energy builds. Have NO expectations concerning what the object will be. It may be mineral, animal, vegetable or human. It could be a rock, a statue, a picture, a building, a squirrel, a crystal, a constellation—or anything in or out of the world.

For instance, if you get an image like the Victorian Waterfall in Africa, do not assume you have to go to Africa and sit there for 30 days contemplating the waterfall! My client who received the prowling tiger image did not go to the zoo; rather, she found a window sticker that served the purpose.

Be creative when an image comes to you. Do not let the object you receive overwhelm you. Use practical terms and look for an object that you can manage to work with for 30 days.

This object holds the positive energy of your new life and the new DNA. It will empower you to make the necessary alterations in your energy field. Keeping a power object in your energy field for 30 days will support the changes immensely.

If you have tried meditation and the above breathing exercise and still receive no image about the energy object, take a break for a day or two. If you are working with a partner or healer, the partner may receive the image of the object.

Pay close attention to your dreams. The image may come to you in a dream. If you do not

remember your dreams there are several methods you
can follow that will help:

    a. Before you go to sleep, set a conscious
decision to remember your dreams.

    b. Have a pen and paper beside your bed to
write down snippets of the dreams you
remember immediately upon awakening.
Talk about your dreams with someone
else, or just speak aloud. This reinforces
the memories and brings forth further
details.

    c. When you awaken, **do not move, get out
of bed or shift position**. As you wake,
immediately review in your mind what
you have just dreamed. Trace the dream
back as far as you can. Try to recall the
dream before the last one and perhaps
other dreams from earlier in the night.
You'll be surprised by how much you can
remember if you don't move.

Step 3: Tasks Assigned by Spirit

The third step I most commonly receive is for
the client to perform some physical act that will alter
something in their environment **in order to reset a
physical space**. It does not have to be huge, like
moving your home; sometimes a simple task such as
rearranging the furniture will help.

One client was asked to play his piano three
times a day for 30 days. This task would definitely
reset the energy in his physical body, as well as in all
parts of the house that could be reached by the
sounds.

Another client was asked to build a medicine wheel in her yard. In connection with the poverty issue in my family (*Poverty Consciousness* and *Slavery and Survival* Chapter VIII), I was asked to go out and buy something gold as a reassurance of my security. Another client with a poverty issue was asked to donate money to a worthy cause every week for a month. This would establish, in his heart that he had sufficient resources to take care of himself and enough to share with others. All of these tasks had to be accomplished within a 30-day time period.

Check with your intuition regarding whether or not a physical task is necessary or helpful for resetting the energy in your body or your life. Your ancestor and your spirit guides will help you discover what this may be. The physical act of creating a garden, taking care of a plant, playing an instrument, moving furniture or doing something physical will fill that energy gap left by the loss of negative energy.

There may be something else your ancestor or guides want you to do. Listen closely to your intuition. Do not be discouraged if you don't hear anything right away. If the session has been particularly draining, you may be tired. If neither you nor your healer receives guidance about how to set your task, take a break and be patient.

Again, the answer may come in your dreams. Pay close attention to your dreams in the next day or two. Otherwise, meditate and see what answers come to you during this quiet time.

If you still get no answers about setting the energy, just feel what your body wants to do. Do you feel like gardening? Do you want to play baseball? Do you want to rearrange the pictures on your walls, the rugs on the floor, make a staff or other sacred object? Follow your instincts in doing a physical task. You can always consult a Certified Ancestral Lineage Clearing specialist if you cannot resolve this issue on your own. Go to *www.AncestralLineageClearing.com.*

Step 4: Follow your Intuition

The above three steps are the ones I most generally use when I take clients through the Ancestral Lineage Clearing Ceremony. This does not mean these are the only ways to reset the new energy. **It is critical that the new energy be set in your physical, emotional, mental and spiritual bodies immediately.** I recommend following these guidelines if you are just beginning to work with energy or are not an experienced meditator (i.e., at least 10 years).

If you are an experienced meditator, intuitive, or healer, and have worked with energy for many years, your ancestor and your own spirit guides may give you other directions to set the energies into your PEMS (physical, emotional, mental and spiritual) energy bodies. Follow your intuition in setting the new energy into your life. Be sure to establish a new pattern for at least 27 to 30 days so that it holds and maintains in all your PEMS energy fields.

Please be sure your instructions come from a guide that has your highest good at heart. Ensure that you are clear about their directions and instructions concerning what actions to take. **When in doubt, consult a professional.**

WARNING: If you receive an instruction that puts you in physical, emotional, mental or spiritual danger or at risk, STOP! No beneficent spirit will ever ask you to take an action that will put you or another at risk, nor would it ask you to take an action against your moral or instinctive principles, especially when it comes to setting positive energy in your field. If the instruction does not feel good to you, then exercise your good judgment and free will and do not follow it.

Closing Prayer

Once the new energy pattern has been set, the Ancestral Lineage Clearing session is complete. It is now time to close the ceremony and thank the Spirits for their assistance in helping you to a brighter and happier future.

Keep in mind that you should use the same tradition in the closing prayer you used in the opening prayer. The closing prayer should end the ceremony in the same manner and form that the opening prayer opened the ceremony.

For closing, if you used the Ho'oponopono Pule, the Hawaiian spiritual traditional prayer recommended in Chapter X to open the session, it can also be used as the closing prayer:

Divine creator, father, mother, son, daughter as one . . .

If I, my family, relatives and ancestors have offended you, your family, relatives and ancestors in thoughts, words, deeds and actions from the beginning of our creation to the present, we ask your

forgiveness . . .
**Let this cleanse, purify, release, cut all
the negative memories, blocks, energies
and vibrations and transmute these
unwanted energies to pure light** . . . **And
it is done.**

This prayer works beautifully as both an opening and
closing prayer.

In my tradition, since I called in the four
directions, the ancestors, our spirit guides and
Angels, my closing prayer thanks all the spirits I
have called in for their support. Then I release them
and send them home.

You may use whatever closing prayer is
appropriate in order for you to feel balanced and to
have closure.

Conclusion

Setting the new energy in your physical,
emotional, mental and physical bodies is a **critical
part of changing the family pattern**. It takes 27-30
days to change a habit, and family patterns are
definitely habits. The old negative family pattern can
return and be re-established if you do not set the new
energy promptly. It is also possible to pick up
negative energy when you are vulnerable.

There are three ways to set the new energy
permanently:
1) Reciting a series of affirmations;
2) Carrying or using a special object; and
3) Engaging in a physical task.

There may be other methods that your intuition, spirit
helpers or ancestor may guide you to perform that

will help set the energy that is right and effective for you.

Chapter XIV
Conclusion

Concluding Remarks

If I could craft a tool box of healing aids for adults and children to help them through life, I would include a process to heal Family Patterns such as Ancestral Lineage Clearing. There are many benefits in altering stubborn and persistent challenges in our lives. Families are our greatest gifts and also provide some of our great challenges.

I hope you have found this book to be helpful whether you use it for your own personal challenges or in your capacity as a healer for others. I believe we are all healers. We heal ourselves and we heal those around us by our thoughts, prayers and deeds.

Every mother heals her children when she bandages a skinned knee and kisses it. Every father heals his children when he puts them to sleep and kisses them good-night. A sister heals when she listens to her sister's broken heart. A brother heals when he mends his brother's broken bike.

Our ancestors loved their families as we love ours. Their decisions may have unwittingly caused disruption in their families but they are more than willing to correct their mistakes, just as we are. Their love heals us as our love heals others. It will always be so.

Below are some comments received from clients who have experienced Ancestral Lineage Clearing firsthand.

Testimonials:
Learning about the story of who the ancestors were, the issues they faced, and the pivotal actions they took has led to a much greater understanding of the truth of how and why those of us in the immediate family relate as we do, act out the current roles, and, most of the time, unconsciously deal with the ancient ancestral issues of trust and love as we do. The Ancestral Lineage Clearing breaks the vibrational link with which the cellular memories are passed forward through the generations.   It is an extraordinary process and I am very grateful to Ariann for her skill and awareness, as she guided me into the understanding of discovered truths and compassion for my family and myself.
A.W., Bend, OR

I did not understand the power held over me by my ancestral lineage until I worked with Ariann. My life has changed, I am changed. I am now doing exactly what I wanted to do, with no restrictions.
Heather P., Santa Fe, NM

Ancestral Lineage Clearing made me aware of issues which have affected our family for generations . . . it has enabled me to see my family members without a lot of the old emotions that got in the way of healthy relationships with them.
White Hawk, PA

"Ariann's ability to safely guide me to and through the source experience blocking my financial prosperity was wonderful. The next day, my view about myself and money was profoundly different. Almost immediately I found myself requesting payment for services, where in the past I would have given those services away. Her Ancestral Lineage clearing is very powerful."
Reverend Misa, The New Dream Foundation

I did not understand the importance of Ancestral Lineage Clearing until I worked with Ariann. I now know that clearing the past ancestral influences is of tantamount importance in order to live a life in true freedom. I honor your work, and I thank you from my heart.
H.P, Santa Fe, N.M.

I became interested in an Ancestral Lineage Clearing session after I listened to Ariann discussing this process. After my session at first I did not think anything was happening. Slowly over the next few days there was a profound shift. It was the most interesting healing experience I have received in the last five years. I experienced a huge energy shift, which has given me a new perspective and freedom to choose a different path. Challenges that kept repeating themselves

*have stopped and new positive energy has
entered my life.*
Barbara F, Cottonwood, AZ.

*During Spirit Quest 2008, Ariann offered an
Ancestral Lineage Clearing. I was stuck on
something that I knew related to either a past
life or ancestral issues. As Ariann guided me
during the session it became clear what the
issue was and I experienced immediate peace
and healing as the energy shifted, giving me a
new perspective and freedom to move
forward with an understanding of what had
previously been blocking me. Thank you,
Ariann, for this profound work.*
Krystalya Marie', Sedona, AZ, *co-author of
the best-selling book series, "Wake-up . . .
Live the Life You Love," with Wayne Dyer,
Deepak Chopra, Mark Victor Hansen,
and author of the "One-Minute Energy Tune-
up" book series.*
http://www.OneMinuteEnergyTuneUp.com

*Many thanks to Ariann Thomas for the
experience of Ancestral Lineage Clearing. I
found myself going on a journey deep within
that was very interesting and created insights
into issues I have had for many years. I am
very glad to learn of some of the reframing
techniques she uses to help with the clearing.
It was very beneficial.*
Jennifer Molton Kellogg, Cottonwood, AZ

Glossary of Special Terms

A

Affirmation--positive statement or declaration of a truth or the existence of a desired goal is within reach. Affirmations are always positively stated, in the present tense, dealing directly with the positive lesson learned and affirming the ability to create a new life.

C

Choice Point—in the Ancestral Lineage Clearing Session during the journey in the past at the ancestor's death bed, the Choice Point is a pivotal point in the ancestor's past life where the ancestor chooses an alternate reality and begins living in the other reality and altering the outcome of the original life and creating a new life for the ancestor and their descendants.

Chronic Illness—after an illness, injury or trauma passes beyond the acute stage. At some point it becomes in the health profession terminology 'chronic' which means not only long lasting but causing a long term change in the body chemistry and/or functioning.

Clearing space—cleansing and purifying old energy and leaving a positive or neutral space for energy work or for living.

D

Dis-ease—the body or one of its systems is not at ease, in a state of less than wholeness and wellness.

Dysfunctional—failing to perform the function that is normally expected, or in a social context; relating badly.

F

Family Karma—the total effect of the actions and conduct carried from past lives into the present lives of family members that have spiritually agreed to work on resolving these issues together in this lifetime.

P

Probability Stream—alternate streams of time/dimensions where realities may/have change(d) based upon different choices made in each significant moment of our lives.

S

Safe space—a term for a confidential setting where one person holds another in a physically, emotionally, mentally and spiritually protected place so a client can be totally open and free with their thoughts, words and actions without fear of judgment or repercussion. Oftentimes safe space is sacred space when prayers and the protection of the Divine or guardian spirits is invoked.

CPSIA information can be obtained
at www.ICGtesting.com
Printed in the USA
BVHW070034160223
658577BV00006B/455